Getting away
with it

52 brilliantideas

one good idea can change your life...

Getting away with it

Short cuts to the things you don't really deserve

Edited by Steve Shipside

CAREFUL NOW

Let's be grown-up about this.
We in the Getting Away With It
team do not advocate cheating,
lying or breaking the law.
Tucked away amidst the tongue-
in-cheek humour of this book
are a surprising number of truly
terrific tips for saving money,
looking better than you do, and
getting the most out of life
without putting in the hard
graft. That doesn't make it an
instruction manual for living.
You, and you alone, are
responsible for your actions.
See a financial adviser before
taking financial decisions; see a
doctor if you think you have
reason to be concerned about
your health. We are happy to
provide food for thought, but
we accept no liability for your
life and no we don't have any
money so there's no point suing
if you break the number one
rule of Getting Away With It by
getting caught out.

Copyright © The Infinite Ideas Company Limited, 2006

The rights of the contributors to be identified as the
authors of this book have been asserted in accordance
with the Copyright, Designs and Patents Act 1988.

First published in 2006 by
The Infinite Ideas Company Limited
36 St Giles
Oxford
OX1 3LD
United Kingdom
www.infideas.com

Reprinted 2006

A CIP catalogue record for this book is available from the
British Library.

ISBN 1-904902-54-5

Brand and product names are trademarks or registered
trademarks of their respective owners.

Designed and typeset by Baseline Arts Ltd, Oxford
Printed by TJ International, Cornwall

Brilliant ideas

Faking it

Rescuing a bad situation

Getting rid of evidence

Put your feet up

Mind over matter

Introduction

Getting away with it (GAWI) is not an exact
science, it is not an art, and it is not a sport.
Instead it is a delicious cocktail of all three, and
true chancers (or 'jammy gits' as they are sometimes known) take
great pleasure in blending their art and their knowledge in order
to play the game. The result, pulling off some coup or other,
provokes a curious mix of envy, mild resentment, and admiration
amongst the rest of us who trundle through life paying full price,
missing out on specials, putting up and shutting up.

This made us stop and think here in the Infinite Ideas offices. Of
course a great deal of getting away with it is down to charm and,
above all, confidence, but at Infinite Ideas we are great believers
that information is actually the ammunition with which to win
life's battles and that even charm and confidence can only get
you so far. As publishers of books of advice on everything from
sex to finance, it occurred to us that, together, our pool of
authors formed a cavalcade of chancers, a smorgasbord of smart
Alecs and a rich source of GAWI expertise. So we asked them all
to chip in with their tips on picking the finer fruits in life – the
ones you know you don't really deserve.

Back in the 1950s Stephen Potter entertained the world with his works on One-upmanship ('how to win life's little games without appearing to try') and Gamesmanship ('the art of winning games without actually cheating'), in which the fictitious Yeovil College of Lifemanship educated its students in the fine art of getting away with it. Students at the Yeovil College of Lifemanship were untroubled by the complexities of email, texting, office politics, flexiworking or fake tans but it's nice to think that if they were to find themselves confronted by the modern world then *Getting away with it* is the kind of textbook they would turn to for advice.

Acknowledgements

Infinite Ideas would like to thank the following authors for their contributions to this book: Charlotte An, Phil Anderer, Linda Bird, Kate Cook, Artful D., C. Ducer, Paula Fastone, Andrew Holmes, K.N. Ivor, Giles Kime, Faye Kerr, Ken Langdon, T. Leaf, I.M.A Lyre, Connor Mann, John Middleton, Jamie D'Odger, Marcelle Perks, Sly Perry, Tim Phillips, K. Rafferty, Dee Seever, Steve Shipside, Linda Stratmann*, Sue Windler, Vincent Wong. Some names have been changed to protect the guilty.

*Linda Stratmann is the author of *Essex Murders, Chloroform: The Quest for Oblivion and Gloucestershire Murders.*

Life in the fast lane

1. Getting upgraded

Do you watch with envy as fellow passengers get the upgrades while you always seem to be stuck in cattle class? Here are some dos and don'ts if you want to turn left as you board.

Getting upgraded on a plane is seen as one of the great perks in life and there are some people who get away with it more than others. The sad truth is that check-in staff know every trick in the book when it comes to upgrade blagging so it's vital to get the basics right.

Defining idea...

'Broadly speaking, human beings may be divided into three classes: those who are billed to death, those who are worried to death and those who are bored to death.'
WINSTON CHURCHILL

Do dress well. That doesn't have to be a suit and tie; just casual smart is fine. Remember that upgrading people means putting them in an exclusive area with others who have paid to be there and so they won't want to upgrade you if you look like a bum.

Do travel light. Carrying small (and preferably expensive) hand luggage makes you a more likely upgrade candidate than someone with a fistful of plastic bags or something that should really have been checked in anyway (which will always have already got you on the wrong side of the airline staff).

Don't tell them it's your honeymoon. It's not quite clear why this so particularly gets up the nose of check-in staff, though we can presume it's because every couple thinks it's worth a go. On two occasions, friends of the Getting Away With It team who really were on honeymoon were turned down. It didn't make things better when on one of those occasions a couple from the Team were then promptly upgraded (and no, we didn't offer to trade places with our friends – this was a long-haul upgrade, honey).

Don't ever try the 'Do you know who I am?!' approach. They are in charge at this point, and should be treated with maximum courtesy and charm. If you were that important then your presence on the plane would already have been signalled to them. This goes double if you are not even famous. Virgin Atlantic once ran an ad campaign about a man pretending to be Richard Branson's brother in the hope of turning left.

Do ask politely if there is any possibility of an upgrade because all things being equal this may be all it takes to decide between you and the person behind you if an upgrade is in the offing.

Be flexible. Fact of life, upgrades are rarely handed out because they love you; they're usually because airlines are among the few businesses that routinely sell the same thing twice (in this case your seat) and express surprise at the subsequent overbooking.

When you check in (nice and early) let them know that you are flexible and can be bumped onto a later flight. They may not seem interested but if there is a chance the flight will be overbooked they will waitlist you and may bump you off it in return for either an upgrade on the next flight or sometimes a financial reward. Best result for the Team was a free two-way ticket on the same long-distance flight plus a night in a luxury hotel. Well worth it for having to suffer an extra day's holiday.

If you've got a good story don't wait until the airport to use it. A friend of the GAWI team was once flying with the latest in entertainment hardware and hence called ahead to the airline's publicity people to 'check' that he could use it in flight. Of course, in the process he was also letting them know he was writing about flying and just wondering…

Here's an idea for you...

Do get a frequent flyer club membership. Every airline has one and your status will be on the screen as they check you in. It doesn't matter if you don't have a gazillion airmiles yet; the point is that you are, or expect to be, a regular customer and this makes you more likely to be upgraded, presumably on the basis that having tasted the fruits of paradise (business class) you might be tempted to fork out for them next time. See if you can sign up online before you show up.

Do remember that not all economy seats are alike. Seats at the front of a row (bulkhead seats in the trade) and by emergency exits have more legroom. Bulkhead seats are normally reserved for those with small children and emergency exit seats only go to those fit enough to open the doors in case of need but if you ask in advance and stress that you are either unusually tall or claustrophobic and less likely to panic when given room then you have a decent chance. In some flights the seat allocation is done on the Net at a set time before take off. Find out if that's the case and sit poised by the keyboard if so because competition is fierce.

2. Burning the candle at both ends

Yes, we all know that being a party animal isn't the path to health and longevity but it doesn't put us off. Until you give up your wild side, try these ways to give your body a break.

Defining idea...

'Be careful when reading health books; you may die of a misprint.'
MARK TWAIN

If we were still in the 1960s, the Free Radicals would be a popular beat combo, but we're not and free radicals are a big problem for such little things. Free radicals are unstable molecules that have lost an electron and are frankly on the rampage until they get another one. In the process they can damage your DNA, attack the collagen layer of your skin, injure blood vessel tissues and generally give our bodies a good kicking, leading to ageing, cell breakdown and eventually even death. Of course they're associated with tobacco smoke, booze, radiation, chemicals and fried food, but they're also part and parcel of metabolism so you're going to get them anyway and, before the health freaks start smirking, excessive exercise and sunshine are also reported to be sources.

This leaves us with the no-surprise news that whatever you enjoy is going to kill you. Great. However, there are ways of giving your body a helping hand to try to minimise the damage.

Your best line of defence against free radicals is a barrage of antioxidants. Antioxidants include the vitamins C and E, plant compounds such as flavonoids and beta carotene as well as some elements such as selenium and copper. Green tea is often held up as a miracle antioxidant and milk thistle and artichokes are believed to do wonders when it comes to helping your liver detox.

All of the above are best served up to your body in the form of a balanced diet featuring loads of fresh (and preferably raw) fruit and veg. If you're not sure then go for lots of colour – as

Here's an idea for you...

Everyone knows that if you want to look great you must get your beauty sleep – but living the high life often leads to poor sleep patterns and that gives your body even less of a chance to take a break and repair the damage. Sleep is essential to your well being, your looks and, with that, your confidence. Of course you could always resort to sleeping pills but this chapter is presuming your body is getting enough dangerous chemicals as it is. Counting sheep and meditation are great ways to try to seduce the sandman but try a short cut that works for most – a herb called Valerian. It calms you down and promotes a good night's sleep (you'll need about 500 to 1000 mg one hour before bedtime).

a rule of thumb red berries and brightly coloured vegetables are a great source of antioxidants. Plenty of water (a couple of litres a day) will help your body eliminate toxins and help with your energy levels and even your looks by ensuring skin stays rehydrated.

There is no substitute for a good diet, and potions and pills won't bring all the benefits of the same compounds eaten part and parcel with the plants they come from, but you're probably looking for a quick fix here rather than life-style advice so with the above provisos in mind here's a quick recovery solution for those days when the flame at both ends feels like it's starting to melt your middle.

You'll want some powdered vitamin C in the form of magnesium ascorbate (by Lamberts or Biocare; take about 1 gram). Add to that some powdered L-glutamine (Higher Nature recommended, as directed on the box) and some milk thistle complex (Bioforce, as directed on the box). Take this combo before going out – it's a winning formula that helps the alcohol to detoxify by giving your liver some helpful allies to aid it in its work to denature the toxin.

Of the antioxidant vits, you'll want lashings of vitamin C, vitamin A and vitamin E. But if you're going to cheat like this then at least get yourself a good quality antioxidant formula (the Getting Away With It team usually recommends Solgar) rather than whatever no-brand cheapo your chemist has in the bargain bin this week – it's your body after all.

3. Living in the sun: benefits and pensions abroad

Fun in the sun doesn't have to be limited to holidays, even for those on welfare benefits or pensions.

Defining idea...

'Most of the shadows of this life are caused by standing in one's own sunshine.'

RALPH WALDO EMERSON

Every now and again, outraged newspaper editors splutter and bluster about people who are living it up on the Costa del Sol with taxpayer's money. To this, some of us respond: 'cool – how do they do that then?'

Indeed, for many of us a reduction in earnings means it makes all the more sense to head for sunnier climes when money gets too tight to mention. The UK, for instance, has one of the higher costs of living and a relatively strong currency, which means that moving abroad can bring the double benefit of finding yourself with greater spending power in a place where basics are cheaper anyway.

Jobseekers

It's not something that's shouted about but it is possible to qualify for Jobseeker's Allowance while saving money abroad. The powers that be are understandably unwilling to fund jaunts to Ibiza at the taxpayer's expense so it pays to study the criteria closely and make sure you tick every box. You can enjoy the Costa del Welfare but you'll have to be able to show that you're looking for work, not just the good times, if you want to get your benefits.

First off, you have to have registered as a jobseeker at least four weeks before you go and you must be entitled to Jobseeker's Allowance on the day you leave. You have to be actively seeking work up to the day you go, and you must be going abroad in the hope of finding work there. That means that you have to sign up at the local equivalent of a Jobcentre in the country you go to and you have to do that within seven days. That means fewer than seven days from the date you last claimed your allowance in the UK, not seven days from arrival in the country, so be careful not to waste time. Remember that on signing up you're also agreeing to make yourself available for work in that country, so find out what the local rules are on 'availability' before you bin the mobile phone and go on a seven day bender in a beach club. You'll be expected to show that you were actively seeking work, just as you would be if you were back home so keep copies of applications, interview requests, etc.

This doesn't mean you can leg it to Phuket, by the way. The deal only applies to countries in the European Economic Area (EEA), and it's for a maximum period of three months, but with a bit of planning you can do it and get to change scenery for a while, stretch your pounds out further, maybe catch a bit of sun, and, who knows, you could end up finding the job of your dreams in the place of your choice.

Pensions

Pensions are relatively straightforward – if you're eligible for a state pension in the UK but want to retire abroad you can continue to receive that pension as long as you contact the pensions office in advance and intend to retire to one of the countries of the EEA or one of the countries that has a benefit agreement with the UK. There are plenty of those: how do you fancy Barbados, for example, or Jamaica? The full list also includes Cyprus, Malta, Mauritius, the Philippines and the USA so there's something there for pretty much all tastes. Note though that Australia, which used to

Here's an idea for you...

Everyone knows that hard-working ants get their pension rights but even the grasshoppers amongst us may be due more than we suspected. If the travel bug has been your guiding light in life then don't forget that while working abroad you have probably been paying into a local National Insurance scheme. Many of us work abroad and basically wave those payments goodbye when we come to claiming a state pension, forgetting that for countries within the EEA and others with special agreements we can also have that money counted towards a state pension. Find out more at the Pension Service (www.thepensionservice.gov.uk).

have a benefits agreement, no longer does. Four months before you are due to reach pensionable age (65 for men 60 for women) you should get a leaflet about it from the Pensions Service. For more information try the Department of Work and Pensions at www.dwp.gov.uk.

4. Lording it: how to get a title

Lordships and lairdships aplenty are on offer on the Internet. However, getting away with acquiring a title is not simply a matter of flashing the cash and donning your ermine hoodie.

Defining idea...

'Lordship of this or that manor is no more a title than Landlord of the Dog and Duck.'
JOHN MARTIN ROBINSON, Maltravers Herald Extraordinary and co-author of *The Oxford Guide to Heraldry*.

Back in days of yore, getting a title was a straightforward (if usually rather bloody) affair, involving slaughtering dragons/Frenchies/Welshmen etc. and promising not to do the same to the king of the day. Thereafter, those directly descended from a land-grabbing mercenary with the morals of a slavering wolf were entitled to call themselves earl/duke/viscount/baron and assume an air of thorough refinement.

Nowadays, it would seem, if you wish to emerge as the noble butterfly you've always known yourself to be, and (more importantly) insist the neighbours refer to you as your lordship/ladyship, all you need to do is buy a title off eBay or go and Google for 'lordships going cheap'.

So why would you need advice on getting away with that? Simple. It's because most of the 'titles' on offer are either downright scams or flimsy notional titles enabling you nothing. Parting with hard-earned cash for either falls far short of the high standards of the Getting Away With It team. So here's the low-down on how you go about getting a real title without actually having to beg, borrow or steal one from the Queen (she's got buckets of them, but she's very stingy). Principal offers of instant nobility tend to run along these lines.

Here's an idea for you...

Seriously considering buying a Scots Baronial title? Then be aware that according to some readings it is the possession of the hearthstone that defines the Baronial seat and some hard-up but still snooty Barons have been known to sell off the manor but keep the hearthstone, presumably so they can still be called Baron and Baroness when they're living in a two-bed flat in suburbia. Don't make a move until you've checked.

English/Irish manorial lordships for sale: True – the English, being a capitalistic lot at heart, separated the lordship from the land and made it possible to sell titles. Being a 'lord of the manor', however, absolutely does not mean being a lord and is a bit of a swindle because it doesn't imply any nobility, merely land ownership. Being a lord of the manor doesn't mean you get to sit in the House of Lords (even the real ones aren't guaranteed that any more), and you certainly won't have lots of forehead-knuckling peasants just waiting to pay you tithes – whatever the nice man tells you.

If you are seriously tempted by the offers of 'lord of the manor', do remember that they don't represent nobility, merely ownership of a property, and that you can't call yourself Lord or Lady whatever. In fact, precisely the same status can be gained, for free, by changing your name by deed poll from John Muck to Lord John Muck (much as Duke Ellington, who never, as far as we know, slaughtered anyone for the king). Bear in mind that it's against the law to do this with a view to profiting by deceiving others; but, that said, if anyone is gullible enough to give you, say, a better restaurant table because of your name, and you didn't lie to them about it, you're pretty safe.

Buy a bit of land and you'll be a Scottish Laird: True. Much like the above, really, and often sold at very reasonable rates as a bit of a giggle for a birthday present. And why not? Still doesn't mean you get to call yourself 'Lord', though.

Irish Baronages for sale: Make your apologies and leave. It's not that Irish Feudal titles aren't legit – many are very ancient and noble – it's just that unlike their Scots counterparts (see below) the records and registration process is not highly rated, making Irish Feudal titles a rich picking ground for con-men.

Scottish Baronages for sale: This could even be the real deal because Scots Baronial titles go with the land not the family. Buying the Baronial seat pretty much gets it for you. However, with legit deals, the price reflects that.

Membership of the most noble order of the …: Only fools and horses – and, according to folklore, Americans – actually believe that memberships of the Ancient and Most Honourable Order of Ferret-Wranglers means anything more than the fact that you've just paid for a piece of paper you could have printed yourself.

5. Getting on the list

Ligging – the fine art of hanging out with the high and mighty – has been going on for as long as there has been a guest list. Why not join the party?

Try this simple experiment. Put up a velvet rope between two small brass posts and position an ape in a dinner jacket in front of it. It doesn't matter if said rope is

Defining idea...

'Seek and you will find. Knock and the door will be opened.'
(Ligger's) Bible

15

guarding nothing more exclusive than a public toilet – sooner or later someone is going to turn up and claim to be on the guest list.

Short of being an internationally recognisable superstar (and even they get turned away sometimes) there are basically two ways of being waved through the rope/ape set up: brandishing an acceptable pass or being a name on the list.

There are passes, and passes. The holy grail of passes is the near mythical Access All Areas (or AAA to initiates), which allows the bearer to go anywhere – including on stage in the case of concerts. AAA passes are pure gold and usually laminated with security devices including photo ID and even holograms to ensure they're not going to be faked. So, unless you're a pro, that's not a likely option.

What is more of an option is the backstage pass, press pass, or a name on the guest list. Of these, the guest list name will almost certainly only get you into the public area. That may be good enough as it will mean seeing the gig for free or hanging with the celebs at the bar but it won't get you into VIP areas. For those you either have to be Brad/Angelina, or look like Angelina (nope, sorry, Brad won't do) and dress like a groupie. It's a sad fact but as long as security remains a male preserve it will be easier for attractive female liggers to get past the rope. If you're a male then you can either consider drag or waiting for the first all-gay bouncer company to start policing gigs.

One of your best bets is to break the lig down into two stages. The first is just to get into the venue; the second is to get into the VIP area. There are a couple of strategies for step one. Try calling the organiser and applying for a press pass. You'll need a decent cover story for this, though, so stick to claiming freelance status for the more obscure magazines or websites because *Hello* and *OK* staff are known by promoters. The other alternative is to remember that every big event involves a lot of little people. They may be caterers, technicians, PAs or drug dealers but they are essential and will be waved through. So become one, befriend one, or pretend to be one.

Once past the rope, head for the VIP area. If that's a small and select group then you're back to the Brad/Angelina deal but if, as is so often the case, corporate hospitality has a hand then you're in with a chance because this means passes with no names. Often this

Here's an idea for you...

Call the promoter with a credible story about covering the party/event for a website or magazine, as already mentioned, but make sure you stress that you will be photographing or videoing the action. Further stress that this is for an extremely hip, live streaming/podcasting/cutting-edge online technology to explain why you only require a tiny handheld digital camera (unless you want to haul around a battery belt and shoulder a TV camera). By getting across that you need a photographer pass rather than a normal journalist pass you ensure that you will have access to the celeb area and/or the pit in front of the stage.

is a disposable wrist strap, a more colourful version of the ones used to tag hospital patients. If you can find out in advance what kind of tag is being used (see who has got corporate invites and ask them) you can get hold of one yourself.

If you have an insider (someone else who was invited and has a tag) then you can always try the toilet switch. Depending on how strict security is, the tags are usually checked on the way into the VIP area but not so much after that. If a tag holder makes a big point of chatting to security on the way in, but pops out again for a minute it is unlikely they will be checked the second time. This means that they can transfer the tag to a mate, who makes his entry shortly after. This has worked for the Getting Away With It team at events including music awards.

Get yourself a quality insider who works for promotions companies or marketing (event sponsors are a rich vein of invites) and you could be sorted long term.

6. Short cuts to supermodel looks

Yes, yes, we know – the key to looking great is lots and lots of sleep, eating well, working out daily, good skin care etc. Surely there must be an easier way.

Defining idea...

'Grace in women has more effect than beauty.'
WILLIAM HAZLITT

The problem is that you haven't quite found the time for all that healthy living stuff but what you do have is a date/party/wedding and just a few hours to get ready. To heap up the pressure, you just *have* to shine. It's an emergency. Like your ex is going to be there and you have to make him jealous, even though he's going to be with the current squeeze – who happens to be Angelina Jolie. What to do?

As they said in *Reservoir Dogs*, it's time to go to work. First things first: first impressions do count, so make sure that you have all your necessary maintenance done for your special night out – hair and nails looking great. It's not just the look itself, it's the fact that the psychological boost will leave you with a glow that shows. For a small investment that goes a long way, a manicure is a must.

A full afternoon in the beautician's is the best way to go but if time and money don't permit and you simply have to polish up your crowning glory then the cheat's way to a shiny head of hair is Aveda's Purefume Brilliant Spray On For Hair (www.aveda.com). This adds instant gloss and shine to even the dullest locks.

The best way to great skin is a healthy diet and a couple of weeks in fresh air, sea and sun (not forgetting your SPF, natch). However, we're presuming that for you this is just wishful thinking so wipe the McDo remains from your mouth and resort to a facial for short-term cheating. If you can afford the time and the money for a salon-based treat then do so – the more you spend, the better you'll feel. However, if you can't, there's plenty you can do at home. Forget cucumber slices on the eyes – it'll make you feel too much like a distressed divorcee and not enough like a sex kitten. Instead go for the likes of Origins Clear Improvement (www.origins.com), which is a black charcoal mask to draw out pore-clogging impurities, followed by an Elemis Fruit Active Rejuvenating Mask (www.elemis.com).

Remember girls (and boys) to have a hot bath before you go out to plump out your complexion with all that steam and to get the circulation going so that you appear rosy and, therefore, healthy.

Nutrition is a long-term thing but there are certain short-cutting cheats that will give you an instant hit of feel-good factor. Try taking a slug of supergreens, for instance. Supergreens are ground up superfoods – extremely health promoting vegetables, algae and sprouted grasses – which give a shot of optimum nutrition in one glass. Upside: you'll swear you can actually notice the difference in energy levels and well-being. Downside: they tend to taste disgusting. So, mix these life-giving powders with a little juice and down the hatch. Two that taste just about OK and give you a spring in your step are Kiki's Nature's Living Superfood (www.kiki-health.co.uk) and Perfect Food by Garden of Life (www.gardenoflifeusa.com).

Depending on how fit you are, some people also recommend performing a couple of press ups (yes that's for girls as well as boys) to flush the blood through your system and bring a healthy glow to your skin. Remember, though, healthy glow should not be confused with out of breath and beetroot faced. Before you make your entrance, try spritzing your face with a water spray, which helps cool you down and also freshens up your make up – so carry your own supply with you at all times.

Here's an idea for you...

Ignore Bridget Jones's nightmare, the gruesome fact is that granny gripper knickers (or 'pants of steel' as India Knight puts it) are the short-term solution to waistline emergencies. On this one, it's only right to go with the advice of India Knight herself (nothing nasty meant by that, India) and get yourself the ultimate pair – Nancy Gantz BodySlimmers High Waist Belly Buster. They are simply the best and the only trick they miss is that they should come complete with a suicide pill on the basis that obviously it is better to die than to let anyone know that they're what you're wearing.

7. Fashionista freebie

Designers happily hand out their best bling to celebs having a night out on the town, but what about the rest of us? How can we dress beyond our means?

Celebrities don't have to pay for Dior dresses or Jimmy Choos because the likes of Dior and Choo are happy to hand over the glad rags in return for the endorsement of their products. You or I, on the other hand, are expected to fork out a fortune for the same things. If you have fashionista aspirations but burger-flipper finances, then you're going to have to adopt some different tactics if you want to doll yourself up at knock-down prices.

The first trick is consider if you might still have some celebrity factor even if it's not exactly 'A' list. If you're going to be photographed and that photograph is going to be published then you are an immediate billboard. While you might not get the front cover of *Heat* there are local suppliers for whom the middle pages of the local newspaper are realistically just as interesting. So give a bit of thought as to who you might appear in front of or be photographed by, and then try calling a small designer who might want to get noticed by those people. Remember to make it crystal clear that you are asking to borrow the items just for that one event, and that you are taking responsibility for cleaning/damage etc.

Before you call take the time to consider and write down the case for what the lender stands to gain. Be realistic about what you can get – you're going to be hard pushed to blag a Chanel evening dress but if it's promotional t-shirts or specialist wear (surfing clothes at a sports event, for example) then you have a chance.

Slightly further down the slippery moral slope is the much used but little talked of tactic of abusing the shops' return policy. Fewer and fewer shops will give you your money back these days if you return an item, but even those that don't will give you an exchange for the full value. If you're shameless enough this means you can effectively use them as a lending library for fashion, returning an item the next day and redeeming it against the next in your wish list. Do remember to check the returns policy of the shop, to keep the receipt, and don't forget that if someone at the soiree spills red wine on you, then congratulations, you just bought it.

Here's an idea for you...

Unlikely as it may seem, many people swear by the charity shops for designer labels. The trick is to find those in the right kind of areas where people dispose of clothes because they are last season rather than, say, because the bum is hanging out of the trousers. Such people tend to give the items away rather than binning them. Hence, rootling around the Oxfam shop in Chelsea, for example, is more likely to bring results than grubbing through the racks in Grungeness.

A slightly less dodgy way of making your hard-earned diva dollars go further is to join a real lending library of to-die-for divaware. Take handbags, for example. If you want to be seen with the most luscious piece of arm candy then you can fork out the cost of a semi-detached house in return for a couple of scraps of leather from Luis Vuitton. Or you can sign up for 'Be A Fashionista' at www.be-a-fashionista.co.uk. For a fee you join up and you are then free to pick a handbag from a range of designer must-haves, which you use for as long as you like. When you fancy another, or simply can't be seen dead with the same one (daahhling), then you swap it for a different one from the selection. There are three different levels of membership, depending on the exclusivity of the bags you're after. The choice starts with 'Diva In Training' from less than £30 a month. For that you get the likes of Antik Batik or Jamin Puech. Moving up in the world you can join the 'Style Guru' level (Prada, Fendi) or splash out for the full-on 'Fashionista' class (nearly £100 a month) and prance around with Marc Jacobs, Dolce & Gabbana or Luella.

8. Free wheels

Yes, you all like the idea of driving a flash car for free. You just don't know what to do about getting one. Until now, that is.

First up, be realistic about who you are and what you're going to get. Aston Martin is happy to deliver a free car to Prince Charles

Defining idea...

'O bliss! O poop poop! O my! O my!'
MR TOAD, *Wind in the Willows*, on seeing his first shiny motor car.

because he's first in line to the throne. Arnold Schwarzenegger gets as many Humvees as he can handle because he represents the kind of biceps-for-brains meathead they want to appeal to. You and I, on the other hand, get test drives ... if we're lucky.

Cars are expensive. For those of us who don't spend our hard-earned cash on subterranean missile silos or private Caribbean islands, the car is usually the second largest expense in your life after your house. The bad news is that nobody is about to hand you a free Porsche; the good news is that you can get to play with wheels beyond your price range.

The most common way people get a spin in fancy cars is by applying for test drives. Sadly you can't just turn up at the Rolls Royce dealer and demand an outing behind the wheel. They don't go for that, funnily enough, so it takes a little planning if you want to play with the best toys in the box. The thinking behind test drives is to snare the target market and simply turning up in your best bib and tucker may not be enough to suggest that you are part of that select few. Start the relationship in advance – manufacturers' websites are often a good place to start by requesting information, which means they will send you marketing material and may even offer a test drive. Gen up on the rival makes because you have to at least appear to be in the throes of the decision-making process. When you do get as far as asking for a test drive at the dealership, look smart and act seriously. When you get your token thirty minutes of accompanied drive, look very thoughtful then summon your best straight face and ask if you can have an extended test drive for an evening or a weekend.

Here's an idea for you...

Although it's not actually freewheeling, possibly the best way of being seen in a truly flash motor is to join a classic car club. Check out www.classiccarclub.co.uk. You pay a monthly fee and trade that off for a certain number of days using their cars. The cars are categorised so your fee will go further if you opt for a seventies BMW rather than for that horny sixties Ferrari, but however you slice and dice it you get to be seen in a variety of classy carriages, many of which you simply wouldn't be allowed to rent or able to afford to insure (especially if you're a younger driver).

If you get an unaccompanied drive, use this time to line up your next. Turn up in your test car at the rival dealership and enquire about their line because you are evaluating both. Seeing you in the first car increases your chance of the second one coming your way.

Be very cautious of the 'free car' offers you may see on the web. These are very common and basically talk up the idea that British and American companies are desperate for people like you to drive their cars 'wrapped' in all-over advertising. As with so many tempting offers there is some basis of truth: we've all seen cars painted all over with ads and wondered who pays for what. The free car sites promise that all you have to do to get your hands on a car is be over eighteen, have a valid licence and a driving itinerary that includes lots of high-profile routes. Some of them even suggest that sponsors will not only give you the cars but also pay you to drive them. Likely? Not. Most such sites actually ask for a fee to sign up to the registry of eligible car drivers. You pay your money (around $25 on average), you get to fill in a lot of forms about your driving activity and it seems that, erm, that's it. You can sit around and whistle for all the cars that are going to come your way.

Money, Money, Money

9. Greasing the wheels: the art of bribery

Palm-greasing might not be legal or ethical to our minds, but unless you have the power to change the laws and customs of a large part of the rest of the world, best get used to it.

Defining idea...

'There are places in which the only compliment is a bribe.'
SAMUEL JOHNSON

Small-scale bribery is a way of life in many countries. In some parts of the Arab world, for example, 'baksheesh' (small tips of a few pence for every service imaginable, including having a door opened for you or a light switched on by a man who lurks in the dark all day waiting for just this opportunity) is a norm without which the poorest members of society would be even poorer. By all means hate it, but if you want that light on, you're going to have to pay for it.

Having this type of culture is a way of getting life rolling. In most cases it has some advantages for the briber, because usually it's a way of getting round pointless regulations or inefficient systems. It works for the people who are bribed because, well, they get something extra. If they are public servants (let's gloss over the irony), it often works for the government too, because the authorities can keep the wages they pay low, and keep the people

who enforce the law happy so they don't launch coups, start civil
wars, or get jobs in the private sector.

So while you might not want to offer bribes, you might one day
find that you don't have a practical option.

Point one: you have to know how to take a hint. People
experienced in the art of soliciting payments will rarely leave you
in any doubt when it's the opportune time to pony up. No one is
likely to say 'I'd like you to offer an illegal payment to me please'.
Instead, you may find someone staring at you with a 'why don't
you ask me how much that costs?' look, or declaring unexplained
fines or charges that you're sure the guidebook didn't mention. If
this happens a few times when you are not expecting it, get a
different guidebook – one written by a person who's actually
visited the country rather than the photo library. By all means,
reasonably question the charge (it may turn out to be surprisingly
variable), but bear in mind who is imposing it. That person may be,
for all practical purposes, the law where you are.

Try to establish who is in charge – that is, who can make whatever
problem it is go away, or provide whatever service it is that you
need. You negotiate with this person. Make sure you are clear
about what you need, whether it's not having your stuff
impounded at an obscure customs post or simply service from a
plumber before next May. Try also to be clear about what they

want: for example, if they say there is a fee, check that the 'fee'
really does guarantee the service. Also, the fee might not be
money; they might just want a little of something you have – food,
for example. In some parts of Africa, cheap ballpoint pens can open
doors (not literally).

Don't openly acknowledge that you're paying a bribe, or you may
put the other party in a situation where they have to stick to the
letter of the law, which at best will mean that nothing will happen
for quite some time (possibly for
ever). Just grit your teeth and be
thankful that you come from a
culture where you have the spare cash
to offer. In many societies, bribery,
tipping and giving alms to the poor
are simply different points on the
same scale.

Finally, don't assume that all
foreigners, especially government
officials, are corrupt or corruptible, or
you could end up in serious trouble.
In some cultures, especially in Asia,
offering gifts or financial inducements isn't just illegal, it's also
embarrassing and insulting. Do your research before giving what
we would consider a harmless present. For example, if you offer a

Here's an idea for you...

The dollar is the international currency
of financial inducements. When you're
likely to need to grease some wheels,
carry a few dollars, but don't flash a
wedge of them or you may find that
the asking price inexorably rises to the
value of the fund you are carrying. If
you're going to be in a country for any
length of time, carry local cash in small
denominations – when you offer a
furtive incentive, you're not exactly
going to be given change, are you?

gift to a business contact in China, never do it until after any deal is done, wrap it up plainly, and don't expect it to be opened in front of other people.

10. Pay less: haggle

Haggling is for life, not just for holidays. You'll save money if you adopt the six habits of highly effective hagglers.

Having resigned from the Society of Life's Underpaid Overtippers (don't bother checking for an amusing acronym – there isn't one), the

Defining idea...

'Necessity never made a good bargain.'
BENJAMIN FRANKLIN

members of the Getting Away With It team know all too well some of the curious habits and attitudes we develop around money.

Once, long ago, after a crap meal and contemptuous service in a place that ought to have known better, our response to a 'suggested gratuity' of 15% on the bill was to signal our displeasure by leaving a tip of only 10%. (Using coins rather than notes was the *coup de grâce*, we felt – a social stiletto wielded with devastating precision.) The moral of the story, of course, is that the £20 tip should by rights have stayed firmly in our trouser pockets. So why do we habitually pay over the odds? Why can't we pay what we need to, not what we feel we have to?

Social conditioning aside, much of our reticence almost certainly stems from a lack of tutoring in the art of haggling. So, try the following on for size: they are the GAWI team's six habits of highly effective hagglers. Chances are that you're already adept in at least some of these areas, in which case pick 'n' mix to your wallet's content.

■ Cultivate a pained expression. When the seller mentions a price, give them a clear facial signal that the price is not acceptable. If you're struggling with how this might look, imagine you've just been told by your lovable but overzealous secretary that he has just simultaneously shredded your appointments diary, passport and jackpot-winning lottery ticket. Now look in the mirror ... that expression will do nicely.

■ As well as managing the visual signals you give, keep an eye and ear out for the signals coming back at you. A pause before a reply comes back to you often indicates that there's a negotiable stance being offered to you rather than the bottom line. Really pay attention to the words people use: when people tell you they can't reduce the price 'at the moment' or 'in these circumstances' or 'as things stand', they're actually letting you know that perhaps they could reduce the price at some point or under different circumstances. Press them to find out what these conditions are. For example, if there's going to be a '50% off across the store' sale coming up, maybe you'll want to hold back and take the risk that you can elbow your way to the front of the queue when the sale starts.

■ Research the market. Whatever the price quoted at you, if you can say 'I know I can get it cheaper elsewhere' and can back the assertion up with evidence, there's a good chance you'll get a reduction.

■ Ask questions like: 'Is this the very best price you can offer me?'; 'Have you ever sold this for less?'; 'What does [insert name of company's chief rival] charge for this?'

■ Create possibilities. Salespeople worth their salt should be doing this for you anyway, but it never does any harm to drop in hints and phrases that might move the negotiation along. You know the sort of thing: 'It's still a lot to pay all at once – are there any credit deals going which might mean we could afford to buy now?' or 'Suppose we took half now and half later – would you still guarantee the price?' Questions like these can help to move a bargaining session out of stalemate, so go into your next negotiation armed with phrases along the lines of 'What if...?', 'Suppose we/you...' and 'How would it be if...?'

■ If the item in question is something you really, really want, it might be worth delegating the bargaining to somebody who is emotionally detached. If the reality is that you are so desperate to lay your hands on something, your language and your non-verbal signals will give you away and you'll end up paying top price.

Now the trick with any of the above is to get practising them. Have a go and we'll be very surprised if by the end of the week you haven't saved yourself at least the cost of this already keenly priced book.

Here's an idea for you...

There's an old Chinese proverb that goes something like this: if you want to find out about water, don't ask a fish. Because we tend to approach bargain hunting from a shopper's perspective, we don't always appreciate some of the tactics deployed by sellers. Improve your bargaining powers no end by reading a few books on sales techniques. And if you want to understand how retailers try to manipulate us, you won't find a better book than *Why We Buy* by Paco Underhill.

11. Blagging that pay rise

While some people seem to have the knack of demanding (and getting) pay rises, the rest of us are left pining hopefully for a beneficent boss to smile on us. Well wait no more.

Defining idea...

'The salary of the Chief Executive of the large corporation is not a market reward for achievement. It is frequently in the nature of a warm personal gesture from the person to him or her self.'

J. K. GALBRAITH, American economist.

You haven't had a raise in ages. Problem is the economy is stagnant (isn't it always?) and your boss thinks you're worthless (which, if we're painfully honest, may be true). No matter, a good blagger never lets little things like worthiness get in the way of getting the reward. A good blagger looks beyond the immediate and considers the long term – a lifetime of getting away with it rather than snapping after trifles.

An assistant stage manager working in a theatre once did a bunk with the £100 she had been given to buy props. 'What a mug,' said a more seasoned ASM. 'If she had waited a bit longer she could have gone off with five times that.' So it is in business. It's only the people with no vision who fiddle their expenses for a couple of pints in the pub, or charge for a first-class train fare and sit in second. This is short-sighted in many ways. After all, do you need to impress anybody who sits in standard class?

Keep the big picture in view. Particularly at the start of your career, bear in mind that the rewards of getting to the top are very substantial. Don't whinge about your early salary. Tell yourself that you are investing for the future. Agree to small or no rises and even no promotions for the first couple of years, then go for the big hike when you have something to argue with. You might be better off doing an extra few months at 20k a year rather than causing grief by bellyaching. The eventual return could be well worth it.

Here's an idea for you...

Use recruitment agencies, the Internet and the HR department to work out the top and bottom ends of the sort of salary someone in your position gets. For a rough idea start by taking the salary survey at PayWizard (www.paywizard.org/). Now work out why you deserve to be in the top 25% of the band. When you have a good case, take it to your boss. If you are already in the top quartile, look for a promotion.

When you are going into a new job make sure that they really want you to join them, and preferably have told other contenders that the job is not theirs, before negotiating the salary. Asking earlier has two disadvantages. First, you may discover that there is a big gap between their expectations and yours. At that time you are negotiating from a position of weakness, since they have not yet decided if they want you. Second, it makes you look a bit petty if the salary is the only reason you're taking the job.

Whatever anyone tells you, you can ask for more money at any time. The key here is timing: ask when your value to the organisation appears very high. Do it when you have just brought off a big deal, or organised the district conference or made a useful suggestion for change. Focus on what you have done and what you will do in the future. Use simple techniques of negotiation like saying 'It's only £10 a week' rather than '... £520 a year'.

The same timing works when you're looking for a promotion. Think, act and look as though you are already in the new job. Seek out, and go after, vacancies. The manager of a small sales team in Scotland heard that the manager of a large team in a higher job category had been promoted. As soon as he heard this he telephoned his boss, whom he knew, and asked for the vacant job. We suspect the boss was simply saving the time and stress of interviewing when he agreed but so what? Job done.

12. Playing both ends against the middle

Big multinational Goliaths are chaotic – fact. Here are a few ways to play David, fell Megacorp with a single stone and make double the money you actually deserve.

Defining idea...

'Never give a sucker an even break.'
W. C. FIELDS

It's impossible to overestimate how the vanity of their managers and their own inherent inefficiency make any big organisation such an easy mark. Individuals or small, tightly run enterprises know how to get away with murder when they're dealing with these lumbering corporate giants. All of the following scenarios actually happened.

Taking advantage of change

The most likely time for a company to make a mistake is when paperwork moves from one department to another. It's called a 'stand off'. A stand off also occurs when a manager moves on and another takes over. Let's suppose you're a supplier, big or small, and your main contact point in a big company has moved on and there's a new guy in place. What can you get away with here?

Some suppliers assume that there will be a smooth handover from one manager to another and that the new incumbent will be well briefed on the current situation. This is a schoolboy howler. It's much, much more likely that the new kid in town hasn't a clue what's going on: and that's your opportunity.

The Getting Away With It team once sold a training course to a manager. It consisted of two phases: the writing of the case study and the actual running of the courses. We'd written, delivered and been paid for the case study when the organisation in its wisdom appointed a new manager and the old one disappeared. The Team went in to see the new guy and we were amazed when it became clear that she didn't know any of the history of the course. But we kept schtum and, guess what – we took another order for the case study. Being somewhat concerned that the original material might be found, we changed the names in the case study and the typeface it was printed in, and redelivered this arguably 'updated' version. So, we got paid twice. The new manager then decided that her predecessor had got it all wrong and ordered a quite different course with a totally new case study. We got paid again. You couldn't make it up!

(Incidentally, as you take advantage of the new person in a post, don't go mad by using a line such as 'Your company has promised to go single tender on this million-dollar contract'. Even the most butter-fingered managers are going to check that one with their predecessors.)

You're a building subcontractor who has put in a quotation for twenty bathrooms in an office block. The quotation includes buying and fitting the wall tiles. Then the customer appoints a consultant to supervise the implementation of the contract. During the first meeting the new consultant confirms that you're getting the business and then it becomes obvious that he doesn't realise that your quote included the tiling and that he's going to get someone else in to do it. What do you do? First and foremost, don't move a muscle and don't say a word. Keep still and accept the assumption, but only tacitly. Now as you start to relax, calculate, inwardly of course, just what that's added to the bottom line. Maybe you could be seeing double.

Taking advantage of the competition

For two years a one-woman-band consultancy did a planning job for a big electricity company. The job was phase one of three phases and was very successful. When it came to phase two, the purchasing department forced the responsible manager towards McKinsey & Co to get a competitive quote.

Here's an idea for you...

Have you got a job that involves travelling nationally or, even better, internationally? Then don't forget how the vagueness of a large corporation will not connect the timing of your trip with other events that you might want to attend. That's how people go to Edinburgh during the festival, Sydney during the test match, Beijing during the Olympics, and so on. There's actually a club for professional travellers who play golf. It's called 'Cowface', standing for '**C**ourses **O**f the **W**orld **F**ound **A**t **C**ompany **E**xpense'. Send an e-mail to the publishers of this book for details.

It made no sense at all to change consultants for the second part of the project. The businesswoman knew this and went in at the highest price she dared. The reaction was a telephone call from the company manager. He sounded embarrassed and told her that he had a problem with her price. The woman thought she'd overdone it and started stammering about how she could probably take another look at it. He agreed with this and suggested that she took another person on to the project and made it more of a team approach. The problem, he told her, was that she'd come in more than £200,000 lower than the McKinsey quote. 'I can't take your number in as it is; the purchasing people will laugh me out of court.' So, she took on another guy and charged even more.

13. Thwarting the tax man

Death and taxes are the only two certainties in life, but while you can't dodge the former, there are ways of avoiding the latter.

Notice that what we're talking about here is avoidance, not evasion. To some people tax avoidance is morally

Defining idea...

'Only little people pay taxes.'
LEONA HELMSLEY, New York property developer, shortly before being convicted of tax evasion.

repugnant and a failure to recognise your duty to society. To others it is seen as part of every citizen's duty to avoid paying more tax than you need to. Whichever view you take of tax avoidance, the really important thing is not to confuse it with tax evasion. Tax evasion is a crime, pure and simple, and that means fines and the possibility of prison, neither of which appeal to the Getting Away With It team one little bit. If you live in Switzerland, however, failing to report income in a tax return is not actually a crime unless it involves deliberate falsification of records.

Here's an idea for you...

If you're dreaming of high-tailing it to the sun with all your ill-gotten gains, there are websites set up that detail all of the legal niceties and jurisdictions of the top tax havens around the planet. Try Lowtax (www.lowtax.net), which lists the top thirty destinations from Andorra to Vanuatu and the tax breaks they offer. You can see it as an international travel guide for the well-heeled looking to settle down and live happily ever after with their money. Happy hunting and bon voyage.

You don't have to be dishonest to avoid tax, just savvy. Let's start with your savings. You may have heard of ISAs but if you don't have one you are paying tax on your savings that is totally unnecessary. ISA stands for Individual Savings Account and it's basically immune from taxation. There are two possible parts to an ISA: cash and shares. The ISA itself isn't an investment, it's more of a protective casing that prevents the tax man taking a chunk out of it, so investments in shares, investment funds and corporate bonds will all be tax free if set up within your ISA allowance. There are also two types of ISA: the Mini and the Maxi. The Maxi lets you invest up to £7,000 in stocks and shares and save up to £3,000 in cash but you can only have one Maxi ISA per tax year. The Mini lets you save up to £3,000 in your cash Mini ISA and up to £4,000 in your stocks and shares Mini. You can have two Minis a year so, basically, you're after a Maxi if you're looking to invest over four grand in shares, and a Mini if you're investing less and want to be free to take up an offer from a separate cash ISA provider.

The other smart way to save is pensions of course, since that gets the max tax relief. Don't forget that inheritance tax is another great money-spinner for the government. You pay tax all your life, then what's left over is taxed again when you leave it to your loved ones. However, you can reduce that too by giving away your legal maximum in presents every tax year.

The ultimate in tax avoidance, however, involves that fine old strategy of running away. If you're looking to retire but will still be getting income from the UK then you might want to think about Panama or the Honduran Bay Islands, both of which levy tax only on locally earned income. Alternatively, the likes of Nicaragua and Malta currently have a flat-rate 15% income tax for permanent foreign retirees. Maybe you don't want to retire but do fancy investing in property. New Zealand imposes no transfer tax (stamp duty) or legal costs on the sale of property and you don't pay capital gains tax on the sale of a residential property.

Nothing on earth moves as fast as a government chasing down a tax loophole, however, so double check with local sources before packing your bags and heading for that tax haven in the sun. Before taking any steps to avoid tax have a word with your accountant or independent financial adviser to ensure you stay the right side of current legislation because in this game information is money.

14. Robbing the bank

Are you Butch Cassidy in your dreams? Sadly, the reality is that it's the banks that rob us with their legions of weasely little charges and small print. Time to turn the tables.

Robbing a bank is dangerous and illegal. It has unpleasant side effects like jail and having to hang out with people sporting misspelled tattoos. Chances of getting away with it are relatively slim so what we'd recommend instead is that you get your own back on banks by taking a chunk out of the slice your bank is robbing from you.

Defining idea...

'*Creditors have better memories than debtors.*'
BENJAMIN FRANKLIN

To start clawing money back, the first thing you're going to have to give up is any idea of being a loyal customer. Don't feel bad about it: banks usually reserve their worst rates for loyal customers so there's no goodwill at stake here.

For a start you can stop paying a fee for your current account. It's just not worth it and even when the fee seems fairly painless, it soon mounts up. At £9 a month, for instance, that's £108 a year that you're handing over for nothing. Move to non-fee paying current accounts and make sure they offer you interest when you're in credit and a 0% overdraft (quite common for the first year).

Next up it's time to become a rate tart. Rate tarts are those canny customers who move their credit card debts from one lender to another to take advantage of low- or zero-rate introductory offers. Although the name doesn't sound very flattering, don't worry, it's only the banks that hate us because rate tarts are reckoned to cost the banking industry a billion pounds a year (what a shame!).

Getting away with rate tarting isn't just as simple as transferring your balance to another card; there are a few important things to take into consideration. The first is the amount already on your card. If it's a relatively small amount, you should be careful that the new lender doesn't impose a fee. Balance transfer fees are usually expressed as a percentage of the credit balance, but many are capped at a maximum (say £50). Clearly the larger the amount of money you are transferring, the more important it is to get a capped fee rather than a percentage. Look before your debt makes the leap.

Also watch out for capped credit limits on the card you want to transfer to; there's no point trying to shift a £10,000 balance to a card that will only carry a £500 maximum. There's also the small issue that once your 0% honeymoon period is up then you'll find that the interest rate charged is often higher than cards without the introductory offer. That should worry you less though, for two reasons. One is that, in an ideal world, you will have paid off the debt by then, using the money saved during the interest holiday to help increase your payments to the card. The second is that you have no intention of continuing to use the card after the end of the 0% period because precisely one month before it ends you will have transferred the balance again to another card company offering 0%. You tart.

There are a couple of things to think about when doing this. The first is to ask yourself how good your credit rating is. There's a lot of talk about rate tarts notching up bad credit records if only because you get a question mark over your name every time you undergo a credit check and you get one of those every time you

Here's an idea for you...

Everyone should have a 'tart alert'. Tart alerts are email or text message memory-joggers that let you know when your 0% honeymoon period is about to end. They're useful for credit card transfers, special offers and as general reminders that your bank is planning to cream a bit more money off you in the near future. Reminders are sent out six weeks before the deadline to give you the time to look at your next best move. Sign up for yours from www.moneysavingexpert.com and, while you're at it, take a look at Martin Lewis's excellent range of money-saving tips on everything from store cards to mortgages.

apply for a new card. If you have a good credit rating (which usually means you owe loads but keep paying the interest) you can probably shift every six months. If not you may want to look at the longest 0% rates available (some are over a year) and aim to pay it off before the period ends and you get hit with the punitive rates.

15. Winging it: long haul on the cheap

Budget airlines have changed the way we pay for short-haul flights, but how do you get away with cheap thrills when your destination is a long haul away?

One of the most reliable and long-running ways of getting cheap long-haul flights is the air courier system.

Defining idea...

'No flying machine will ever fly from New York to Paris ... [because] no known motor can run at the requisite speed for four days without stopping.'
ORVILLE WRIGHT

The idea behind courier flights is that in return for accompanying an item of cargo, you get to fly at cut price to destinations that are normally top whack.

The reason why it works is that normal cargo doesn't clear customs as soon as it arrives – instead it sits in a warehouse until it is released. This is fine unless you have an item for which delivery is very time sensitive (important documents, crucial engineering components, or whatever else it may be), in which case you want it to clear customs immediately. It won't do unless it's accompanied – which is where you come in. As a courier it's your 'excess baggage' that's travelling as freight and it will clear on arrival rather than sit in a shed. You don't have to worry about what the consignment is because you are not legally responsible for its contents so you can forget all those nightmare stories about Thai/Turkish jails. Despite whatever you may have seen in the films you don't have the cargo sitting next to you, or chained to your wrist, throughout the flight; in fact, you may not even see the cargo because what you are carrying is the paperwork, not the object.

What you get out of the deal is a flight at a fraction of the cost, often just a quarter of the normal ticket price. To qualify you'll need to be over eighteen, smart in appearance, and with good English. You'll have to register with a courier company and you buy your tickets through them, usually several weeks in advance, collecting the ticket itself on the day you fly.

There are restrictions: usually the only destinations on offer from the UK, for instance, are Tokyo, Bangkok and Sydney, and couriers fly from Heathrow. The flights are either on British Airways services if you're flying for BA Cargo (www.baworldcargo.com) or Virgin if you're flying on behalf of Air Cargo Partners (www.acpww.com). Some couriers have found flights by contacting BA travel shops (tel

0870 606 1133) and booking that way. Do note that it pays to be flexible, smart, and reliable – if you fail to show for a flight you won't find any more coming your way.

One of the best ways of getting the full benefits of flying courier is to join a courier organisation such as the IAATC (International Association of Air Travel Couriers), which acts as a broker between courier companies and couriers. For a small annual fee it supplies lists of routes, cargo companies, and last-minute deals. Contact them via their web site at www.aircourier.co.uk/. If you're flying to and from the US then you might also want to look at an American equivalent such as Courier Travel (www.couriertravel.org), which operates a search engine of courier and standby flights as well as email warnings of last-minute specials.

Here's an idea for you...

'Air miles' have been going since the 1980s and have long been assumed to be the preserve of frequent flyers, so much so that a lot of irregular flyers don't bother to sign up for them. Big mistake. Only about half of the air miles being earned are given away by airlines, the rest come from supermarket loyalty cards, subscriptions to ISPs or welcome deals for signing up to anything from the Lottery to book clubs. Sign up for every loyalty scheme you can, not only because it increases your chances of getting upgrades but also because, even if you don't have a single point, you can still find yourself being sent special offers on flights.

The amount you save will still depend on how in demand seats are on that flight, so flights at Christmas are harder to get and more expensive than during low peak. Regular couriers also recommend keeping an eye out for factors that make normal travellers avoid an area. After the tsunami, for example, flights to Asia dropped to near giveaway prices as tourists abandoned the destinations but business deliveries still had to be made.

16. Beating the bookie

There's a gambling proverb: 'In every bet, there's a fool and a thief'. The thief is getting away with it. Problem is: how do you recognise when you're the fool?

At this point, you're probably expecting a (literally) foolproof scheme to win cash when you gamble, like the sort of things blokes tell you down the pub which seem to make perfect sense, such as continually doubling the money you put on black in roulette, or which cards to twist on in blackjack, or the name of a dead cert in the 3.20 at Sandown. If you've ever taken their advice, and we really hope you haven't tried the roulette one, we can confidently tell you now: you're the fool.

In gambling terms, the key to getting away with beating the odds is to bet big when you have an 'edge' – that is, the odds are slightly

Defining idea...

'*Remember this: the house doesn't beat the player; it just gives him the opportunity to beat himself.*'
NICHOLAS 'NICK THE GREEK' DANDALOS

in your favour – and bet nothing when you don't. It sounds simple, but hardly anyone bets like this. We bet when we think we will win, or when – even worse – we feel lucky.

Luck has nothing to do with this. If you genuinely believe your special lottery numbers mean you are more likely to win the jackpot, get over it. They are just numbers. Gambling is a game of chance.

So compare the odds of winning with the return on offer, and when those odds are in your favour, you're getting away with it. For example, there might be a 50% chance that a horse will win a race. However, if its odds are even money, the bet isn't an opportunity for profit, so don't bet. If there was a 51% chance it would win at the same odds, then you are getting away with it. Spotting the extra 1% and backing it is your edge.

This starts with your choice of game. Lotteries are often a poor bet, with a huge margin for the lottery company, and comparatively few chances to win. If you play the lottery and own power tools, you are about as likely to win the jackpot as to be killed in a bizarre DIY accident.

The clever lottery player will get an edge by buying tickets only when there's a big rollover. If, thanks to a massive jackpot, the value of the prize money being given at one draw exceeds the value of the tickets bought for that draw, you have an edge – even though your chances of winning on a single ticket are still the same … millions-to-one. You might buy lots of tickets for these rare draws, never play the rest of the time, and that's theoretically an edge over the game – though it might take several thousand years to pay off.

The scarcity of a clear edge that no one has appreciated is why a professional horseracing gambler who spends seven days a week on research might make six bets a year rather than six bets a race like you do. Trouble is, as soon as someone else spots that edge and backs it, the bookies cut the odds. The reward is smaller, and so if you don't have a bet on, the edge has gone.

The principle of finding someone less smart to take your bet is why poker, played online or in a casino, is also popular with serious gamblers. You'll know whether you have the talent to play poker and win by following the old poker player's rule: look around the table for the mug. If you can't see one, it's you.

Here's an idea for you...

Check out the Internet betting exchanges. They are popular with smart punters because they offer the chance to find fools. On an exchange like Betfair or Betdaq, you're not making a bet with a bookmaker, you are making it with another individual, and individuals are a much softer touch than a professional bookie. The trick is to spot your fool first. If you want to bet that Manchester United will lose, for example, you might get much better odds from someone who is a United fan, whose judgement is subjective. Betting exchange odds are, in about 80% of cases, better than those you could get from the bookies.

Unlike casino games like roulette (set up to guarantee that the house always wins if you play for long enough), poker is played against other people. Study strategy and apply it with discipline and you have a long-term edge over 'lucky' (translation, 'loss-making') players which they can never comprehend.

Alternatively take the advice of one professional gambler we consulted: 'How do you guarantee you'll make money out of gambling? Become a bookie.'

17. Getting paid for gaming

Getting paid for playing computer games sounds like something a teenager would dream up. Well, it happens, and there's decent money to be made from your keyboard frenzy.

Defining idea...

'After a certain point, money is meaningless. It ceases to be the goal. The game is what counts.'
ARISTOTLE ONASSIS

Of course, technically, anyone who's ever fired up Minesweeper at work has been paid as they played, but there's a very big difference between sneaking a crafty Solitaire session when the boss isn't looking and genuinely playing for profit.

This year, the Cyberathlete Professional League (CPL) is hosting a $1m World Tour featuring nine stops on four continents and culminating in Dallas where the overall champion will pick up $150,000 (£78,000). At the Cyber X Games in Las Vegas, more than a thousand happy fraggers get together to compete for a total of $600,000 (£312,000) of prize money. The biggest name in the business, Jonathan 'Fatal1ty' Wendel, started out as a pro in 1999 by entering the CPL tournament in Dallas and won $4,000 for placing third. He then really stamped his authority in the arena by becoming the world Quake III champion, netting the $40,000 grand prize in the process. He also won the first Doom 3 championship (another $25,000 in the bank) and presently reigns as the only three-time CPL Champion of the Year, winning each annual title in a different game, a feat never before accomplished.

For every Fatal1ty there are dozens of less spectacular winners who are on salaries to play, often sponsored by technology or lifestyle companies aiming to get their brands in front of young males (a group notoriously hard to reach by TV advertising).

Pretty much all of the big money games are fragfests (first person shoot-'em-ups), featuring the likes of Counter Strike, Doom 3 or Unreal Tournament, but now and again a new game is selected, as was the case in 2005 when Painkiller was chosen as the principal platform for competition. A new game often means new opportunities for would-be professionals and in this case the UK's top pro team, Four Kings Intel, staged a *Pop Idol* type tournament, paying expenses for wannabees to travel to qualifiers to see if they had what it takes to tackle the bad boys.

As you may have spotted from the name, Four Kings is sponsored by chip manufacturer Intel. Most pros rely on sponsorship as well as prize money to pay the bills as they work their joystick thumbs to the bone.

According to the manager of a sponsored Counter Strike team in Sweden (one of the first countries to take to pro gaming) the team members usually make about $4,000 a month after taxes; considerably more than the average salary.

Sponsors don't just hand out cash to every slacker who asks for it, so before writing to your likely candidates you'll need to set out your case and just what it is that you are asking for. Are you after a

Here's an idea for you...

It's not just tournament players who play for pay. Remember that all computer game developers have to test their games before they release them, and that means getting people like you in to play them endlessly in the quest for glitches. It's not particularly well paid, but if you're the kind of person who lives for joystick kicks it's still a dream come true. You'll need good gaming skills and a thorough knowledge of that type of game as well as the company's other products but if you feel you have that then apply directly to the developers as a tester.

salary? In this case you're going to have to show that you are a potential world-beater, with the tournament wins to prove it. Even if you're not in that league, however, you might find sponsors prepared to contribute to travel and hardware costs. The key factor is whether you can convince them that this is a cost-effective way of getting their branding in front of their target market. For an idea of how to phrase your sponsorship demands and an example sponsorship contract, make your way to UK Terrorist at www.ukterrorist.com/articles/sponsorletter.

Be careful not to overdo it, mind – a 28 year old in Korea recently keeled over and kicked the bucket after playing Starcraft for 50 hours straight in an Internet café in Taegu. Seems he forgot the need to eat and sleep. Make sure all your deaths are virtual ones.

Faking it

18. Faking being well read

Given that we're still judged by what we read, how do you fake being well read if you've flipped through nothing but porn and Harry Potter since school?

A friend of the Getting Away With It team gets very upset about the fact that, however bad the book, and however good the TV drama, you will always get more cred for having read a book than for watching the TV.

Defining idea...

'Books . . . are like lobster shells: we surround ourselves with 'em, then we grow out of 'em and leave 'em behind, as evidence of our earlier stages of development.'
DOROTHY L. SAYERS

Victoria Beckham ('Posh Spice') once confessed to 'never having read a book' in her life and was immediately ridiculed by all and sundry. She quickly took it back. While it's fair to say that ridiculing Posh is fair game at any time, it's interesting that even bubblegum pop eye-candy can't be seen to be poorly read – it's an admission too far for anyone, it seems. So if your cultural tastes lean more to Spice Girl than Solzhenitsyn then this is what to do.

First off consider what your goal is in trying to pull this off. Are you attempting an all-round performance with a view to creating an aura of sophistication and culture, or are you trying to impress (or simply keep up with) someone who is themselves better read than you. Think carefully because the answer will define your strategy.

If you've never really read anything more taxing than cereal packets yet need to pass yourself off as the bionic bookworm then you're going to have to put in a little bit of legwork. You might even have to read something. Not much, though – that would be missing the point. For a start don't bother with any of the big fat ones (not that you were going to anyway). There are short cuts to cultivating your literary savoir-faire – reading a couple of short poems, for example, preferably in a foreign language, will go a long way.

If you realise you are expected to know a novelist then don't go for the favourites but instead find something short and obscure. Most of the big boys have written the odd short story or novella on the way to fame and the more weird and wonderful the better. Use this to head off any direct questions about the other books you've read. For example, if anyone starts talking about Hemingway's *For Whom The Bell Tolls* you need only nod and mumble something about the seeds for the novels being sowed early in the (satisfyingly) short stories.

The Getting Away With It team's tip for just-add-water intellectualism is to skim a copy of Schopenhauer's *Essays and Aphorisms*, which provides bite-size nuggets barely longer than the jokes in a Christmas cracker. Because they are philosophical musings on just about anything, they are also ripe to be brought out on almost any occasion. Use discretion when doing this, though; the person who insists on coming out with the same phrase over and over doesn't come across as well read, just well annoying.

Good phrases for the bluffer include lots of vague adjectives ('authoritative', 'entrancing', 'hypnotic') and a couple of equally vague themes ('alienation', 'timelessness', 'loss of innocence'). String these together and you're on a winner. Try it. You can sum up anything from Chekov to *Charlie and the Chocolate Factory* as a 'hypnotic study of alienation and loss'.

Here's an idea for you...

Get a copy of *How to Become Ridiculously Well-read in One Evening: A Collection of Literary Encapsulations*, edited by E. Parrott. It's a collection of humorous poems summarising the classics. The odd thing is that, while it is meant as humour, much like spoof history book *1066 And All That*, it nonetheless gives you some great thumbnail sketches of the literary greats and an insight into what a well-read person's reading list should feature.

By the way, if you're pretending knowledge of books you've never read and it looks like you're going to be rumbled, don't forget that even those who really have read the work are unlikely to remember much detail. This is doubly so if they also read hundreds of other books and have been doing so for a long time. So a risky (but very satisfying) strategy is to infer that you read the entire works of an author years ago in your youth when devouring all the world's literature. This is harder to pull off if you're closer to sixteen than sixty but only literature professors can quote chapter and verse from books they've read. There is even a way to reverse this and head off the rumbling. When someone is detailing a precise scene or character, smile fondly and suggest that this freshness is because of their having only just discovered the writer. Then glaze over gently and nod as if casting your mind back to those days when you too were gauche enough to get excited about Gogol or Proust.

19. Bluffing it as a wine buff

A few easily affected mannerisms and a few well-chosen phrases will help you get away with it when you're posing as a wine buff.

Anyone planning to fake it in the world of wine needs to remember just one thing – actions speak much, much louder than words. There are two pieces of simple logic behind this strategy. The first is that there are a few easily performed rituals that will instil such confidence in

Defining idea...

'A good general rule is to state that the bouquet is better than the taste, and vice versa.'
STEPHEN POTTER, father of one-upmanship.

your oenological prowess that neither professionals nor amateurs would ever question the pearls of vinous wisdom that might drop from your lips. The other is that really accomplished wine buffs tend to shroud themselves in a mysterious air of silence – it is only the amateurs who drone on about malolactic fermentation and yeasty autolysis.

Seven confidence-instilling rituals

While the half hour required to practice the following might seem onerous, remember that it can take a lifetime to equip yourself with the knowledge required to be a real wine bore.

Step 1: When picking up a bottle, never look at the label before pouring. This will send out a subliminal message that you are the sort of person who can identify a glass of Chateau Rip-Off at fifty paces. Those who can barely tell red from white should simply sneak a sideways glance a second or two later.

Step 2: When pouring a glass of wine, never serve yourself with more than the equivalent of a double spirits measure.

Step 3: Leaving the glass on the table, place your forefinger and your index finger either side of the base of the stem and gently rotate the glass as though moving it round a ouija board. Your manner should be deliberately casual and slightly distracted and you should talk about some trivial, unrelated subject in the way that surgeons do while performing open-heart surgery on TV hospital dramas. This will give the impression that tasting wine is something that you do all the time – and could happily do in your sleep.

Step 4: Continuing your conversation – and affecting the same slightly distracted manner – hold the glass at arm's length at a forty-five degree angle, ideally holding it in the direction of a source of natural light and frown slightly but don't pass comment. Tipping the contents of the glass over your shoes will obviously give the game away.

Step 5: Next, lift the glass to your face in one swift movement and immerse your nose deep into the body of the glass. Breathe deeply as you would with an inhaler.

Step 6: With another swift movement, sip from the glass and swill the wine round your mouth while gently sucking air between your lips. If you suck too forcefully there's a chance that you will inhale the wine and cough violently, creating a Jackson Pollock style pattern on your shirt, so suck with care.

Step 7: If there is a dedicated spittoon, accomplished spitters can provide a really convincing finale by discharging a fine stream of wine from their lips. (When you are really good, your aim and range should be sufficient to take out a fly on the other side of the room.)

Learning to sit on the fence

A few pre-rehearsed comments will speak far more loudly than a litany of fact and half-baked opinions. Ideally these should be as non-committal as possible (it's always embarrassing to wax lyrical about a wine, only to discover that it was badly corked or mistakenly poured from a bottle that was opened a fortnight beforehand). Remember that wine appreciation is a bit like abstract art – in the same way that one man's paint spill is another's abstract expressionism, one man's vinegar is another's vinous nectar. Also avoid commenting on anything too specific such as its origin, grape variety or vintage – wild guesses will inevitably get you into trouble.

Here's an idea for you...

Take a tip from wannabe rock stars the world over and practice your sniffing and slurping routine in front of a mirror at home. The first stages of spitting practice can be done with water over a hand basin. Remember that even bluffing requires practice.

The following all-purpose phrases can be said about any wine. They will satisfy amateurs and shouldn't raise the suspicions of professionals:

'What a VERY interesting wine.'

'Very cool climate.' [This is worth a punt since almost all good-quality wines are made in cool areas.]

'Amazingly deep colour.' [All wine is an amazingly deep colour.]

69

'It would be interesting to see how it responded to another year or two in bottle.'

'Goodness, isn't it fascinating to compare this with the 1999' (or whichever was the preceding vintage).

20. Photogenic fakes: looking great in photos

You know who they are – the plain Janes and Johns who somehow look like film stars when they're captured on camera. Join them. Get away with looking great when you don't.

Defining idea...

'With charm you've got to get up close to see it; style slaps you in the face.'

JOHN COOPER CLARKE, poet and comedian.

We once read that you can disguise a wobbly chin in photographs by sticking your tongue into the roof of your mouth – it makes the lower facial muscles contract and tightens that little double-chin patch. Get to a mirror and try it ... See? Ingenious, isn't it.

Models and celebrities know all the tricks of the trade – if you watch them carefully at red carpet events you'll catch them strike a carefully calculated pose as the paparazzi gather. So, next time you have to face your public, try some of these tricks picked up from celebrities and photographers.

■ To look your slimmest try standing with one foot slightly in front of the other, and gently pivot on your feet so that your body including your shoulders are at a slight angle. Putting your hands on your hips can make your waist look smaller, so overall it'll take inches off your body.

■ If you're sitting down, just lean forward and rest your elbows on your knees – that way you'll disguise any wobbly thighs and look slimmer.

■ Look lively. Greta Garbo *froideur* isn't always the most flattering attitude to adopt in snaps. In fact, some professional portrait photographers insist the best pictures are always taken when the subject is looking animated and chipper– that way the subject's personality is captured. You can still engineer your 'best side' in front of the camera.

■ Practise in the mirror. Come on, you did this enough as a teenager. If you find a pose you're happy with, it's worth perfecting it, so you can strike it the moment the camera comes out.

■ Brighten up. Dark colours can be slimming to wear, but black can be draining against the face, so choose brighter colours on your top half to bring out the best in your skin tone.

■ Beware brightly patterned clothes, too; they can swamp you and detract from your face.

Here's an idea for you...

Maximise your lips. To pout beautifully, try turning to the camera and say 'Wogan'. Sounds bizarre, granted, but try it. It somehow produces the perfect pout – glamour models swear by it.

■ Dark circles or bags under your eyes? Try lifting your chin – you'll avoid shadows falling on your face.

■ Do smile. Forget looking moody – everyone actually looks more attractive when they're looking happy. Plus a lovely smile really does take the focus away from the bits you're less happy with.

■ Poker straight hair can pull your face down. Putting your hair up can soften your features and draw attention to your smile.

■ Get them to take more than one! The more photos you have taken, the more likely it is you'll be captured from a flattering angle. Remember, safety in numbers.

Make-up tricks

You'd be forgiven for thinking that slapping gallons of foundation and concealer over spots and blemishes would create alabaster skin and produce wonderful photographs you'd display with pride. Forget it: overdo the slap and you'll look like a waxwork – or, worse, a cross-dresser. Instead, be subtle.

■ Apply a light foundation only where necessary – sides of nose, over spots, that kind of thing.

■ To avoid shiny-face, stick to matte formula make-up on your blemishes and only use creamy, reflective concealers on the eye.

■ Flatter your best features – apply blush over to the apple part of your cheeks, sneak a couple of extra false lashes on your eyelids, slick on some glossy lipstick. Don't forget the golden rule of make-up, though: never overplay the eyes *and* the lips – choose between them before you open that make-up bag.

■ Ask for a minute or two before the camera clicks so you can touch up and dab a bit of powder over shiny bits. Who cares if you seem vain – there are few things as insidious as unflattering photos of yourself *in someone else's hands...*

21. Tantastic fake tans

The dappled orange people never cease to raise a snigger in us. Getting away with a fake tan involves more than throwing away the receipt and the packaging.

Defining idea...

'The two basic items necessary to sustain life are sunshine and coconut milk. Did you know that? That's a fact.'
DUSTIN HOFFMAN, as Ratso in Midnight Cowboy.

A tan makes you look slimmer and leaner, by sculpting, shadowing and highlighting muscles and curves. Your legs look longer, you look more glamorous and, most important of all, the boost it gives to your self-confidence will give you that extra edge right from day one of your holiday, not to mention restraining you from dashing out into the sun and becoming the beach lobster. However, sunbathing and sunbeds bring all the joys of skin cancer, premature ageing and that curious barbecued look that only C-list celebrities appear to think is normal.

While it's health irresponsibility to speak well of sunbathing and sunbeds, we can recommend fake tans: they've come a long way. For the best results, have the tan applied in a salon. It will usually last for about five days. If you can't afford that then remember the three golden rules: exfoliate, moisturise, and layer.

Exfoliation is the real key to a convincing fake tan because the difference between natural and ideal colour shows faster the more surface skin rubs off. Take your time over it and keep thinking about how blotches will make you look silly if you get impatient now. Next up is moisturising to give the skin underneath the best chance but don't then rush into application or the moisturiser itself will interfere with the tan. Leave it twenty minutes or half an hour before you start to apply the first layer of colour.

Use less tanning product where your skin is thicker as the colour will stay longer on these bits anyway. To prevent uneven darkening on bony areas like knees, elbows and ankles, remove excess moisturiser with a damp flannel before applying fake tan. Some experts even recommend avoiding self-tanner on these areas altogether.

Then build up gradually using long even strokes. Keep the application as light as possible because while you can always add more layers later you won't find it as easy to remove. Don't just do the bits you think are going to show, do the lot because this is one

Here's an idea for you...

One of the biggest give-aways of the self-applied tan is stains and blotchy tanning on your hands. Take a look and you'll see there are dozens of people who have clearly spent hours getting it nice and even over their legs but have splotches all over their mitts. So don't let it happen to you. A simple pair of polythene or medical latex gloves (not washing up gloves, as you'll lose that delicate touch) is all you need to avoid being rumbled. And if you do get a splash on your hands then try a lemon on it; the best way of removing self-tanning stains.

all-over tan where you don't have to overexpose yourself and anything you miss is truly going to give you away if errant body parts make a break for the daylight. Get a friend to do your back – uneven 'tanning' on the back is a sure-fire give-away – and don't forget to do your feet. When you're done, get the aforementioned friend to check it out for you – peering over your shoulder at the mirror is not good enough. Give them the full twirl in your bathing costume to be 100% sure you are a bronzed god/goddess, not a copper-coloured clot.

St. Tropez is generally regarded as the crème de la crème of fake tans, though there are numerous alternatives on offer. Just remember that whatever you do, go for a 'matte' finish. The alternative 'shimmer' only really suits those who think that fashionable evening wear includes a light dusting of glitter and a boob tube.

The Body Shop once had a campaign in which it declared that 'the only safe tan is a fake tan', which is all well and good but don't forget that a fake tan doesn't itself protect you against the sun. Once you're out there on holiday remember to slap on the SPF with all the care you would if you were exposing your lily-white virginal limbs to the sun – because that's exactly what you are doing.

22. Faking the big O

There are perfectly good reasons to fake an orgasm and a number of tricks that ensure your partner is none the wiser.

Faking it when it really matters is crucial, so we get advice from a real-life porn star who knows more than a thing or two about putting on a good show.

Defining idea...

'I'll have what she's having...'
The lady from another table in *When Harry Met Sally*.

When Julius Caesar said 'Men willingly believe what they wish', he wasn't talking about fake orgasms, but he might as well have been. It can be positively helpful to add a bit of *faux* grimaces and sound effects to help your partner along with their vinegar strokes; you never know it might even just work for you too. Barbara Keesling in *Beyond Orgasmatron* suggests that mimicking an orgasm can fool your body into really having one: 'The main behavioural principle is to choose one physical aspect of orgasm that you can control and over-practise it.' This could include deep breathing, tensing your arms, legs or PC muscles or screaming. We tend to get more boisterous and out of control just before we climax, so be prepared to be vigorous, especially in the pelvic area.

If you're a woman and normally experience G-spot orgasms, accentuate the deeper penetrative possibilities of your sexual position: if you're in the missionary put your legs up as high as they'll go, preferably over his shoulders. If you normally experience clitoral orgasms, then it's more likely that you'll want to get into the woman on top position and grind yourself strategically rather than going for up and down strokes. Getting away with faking it is really about knowing how your body normally responds sexually and aping this action as realistically as possible.

Aural intercourse is also important, as sexual partners have to rely on expressions of ardour a lot to gauge how excited their other half is. If you normally make a lot of noise, it's a good idea to tape yourself moaning during the throes of a real orgasm and play this secretly back to yourself so that you can remember what kind of nonsense regularly comes out of your mouth. If you suddenly start saying 'Oh yes, yes,' when your normal thing is just to make animal grunts, he'll be surprised. The easiest thing is to make a succession of small moans that gradually get louder and deeper in tone. And, of course, when he gets to the point of ejaculation inevitability, he'll be screaming himself and will pay no attention whatever you shout. It's a good idea to make more noise anyway; you're more likely to be able to let yourself go, and an inability to do so is the main reason why people have problems reaching a climax. Faking into the real thing is an obvious plus.

Be careful though, as it is possible to tell when someone's faking it if you know what you're doing. In a telephone interview, US porn star Stormy Daniels (www.stormyxxx.com) admits that around 50% of her screen orgasms are faked. 'It's not a problem with the guy; it's because of the amount of takes we have to do from different angles.' She reveals the most common mistake that fakers make: 'I know for a fact that when most women are actually having an orgasm they usually stop breathing for a second. They get louder and louder and then they get quiet for just like a second and hold their breath. That's a sure way I can tell if somebody's faking it or not. Their body usually tenses up, but they hold their breath, and when they're faking they always forget to do that!'

You have been warned! To fake it right, think of an orgasm as the French describe it: *le petit mort* (the little death). At the moment of your *faux* climax, imagine Dracula has just bitten you on the neck and you are frozen with suspense – aaghh! Yep, you've got away with it. Fade to soft moans and languid movements…

Here's an idea for you...

To make it easier to give a convincing performance, stage the 'climax' scene in a position such as doggy style where your partner is not facing you. It's much easy to make wild noises and grunts when you don't have to look in his eyes and it's much harder for him to detect that cut-off point when you have to stop breathing and get all quiet for a second.

23. Dressing yourself slim – women

If thinking of a hideously strict diet before that date/interview/holiday drives you to the cake tin, take heart. You can look thinner and more elegant through your choice of clothes.

Defining idea...

'I have always said that the best clothes are invisible ... they make you notice the person.'
KATHARINE HAMNETT, fashion designer.

One of the Getting Away With It team used to be rarely seen out unless in black. Neither did her magazine colleagues. 'It's the media uniform,' she explains, 'the one-colour-suits-all for every event in your working life. And beyond, actually. I'd wear it to every function too – weddings, christenings, bah mitzvahs, garden parties. Even at the kind of outings that begged for the most feminine florals and pastel chiffon, I'd be there head to toe in some billowy – or worse, silhouette-enhancing – black number, believing it made me look barely there thin.'

Black can indeed look supremely elegant – the longer the streak you create, the better. But individual it rarely is. Dark colours certainly can minimise the bulges, but it's not the only sartorial route to a more slender you. Besides it can also be dreary, draining and make you look like 'the help'. Get it ever so slightly wrong at functions and you'll have half a dozen coats flung at you, or be asked for another vol-au-vent, both of which, when you're aiming for willowy Eva Herzigova-esque grandeur, will extinguish the joys of appearing to have a slightly smaller arse.

Instead of black, be inventive. Follow these guidelines:

- You can minimise bulges by sticking to one colour – and pretty much any colour. Obviously dark colours are the most flattering, but in summer you can still create the illusion of being longer and leaner if you're dressed head to foot in the same shade, even white.

- When you're shopping, make it a rule to ignore size tags. Don't buy the snug size ten just because that's your usual size. You look can lose pounds by wearing slightly looser clothes which skim over bumps and hang flatteringly.

- Where possible, choose lined clothes. They won't hug you so unforgivingly. Lined trousers are a godsend, particularly in summer because they drop crisply, however hot and sweaty you are beneath.

- Invest in an A line skirt. It flatters almost everyone because it doesn't cling to your curves, and it minimises your bottom. The best length is on, or just below the knee – and if you team it with knee length boots you can disguise thick legs and hefty unfeminine thighs. In the summer a light coloured skirt can look great with suede or denim boots.

Here's an idea for you...

Colour experts say white, silver and mother of pearl are 'eternally feminine' because they're associated with the moon, stars and sea. Remember that luminous uber-gown that Nicole Kidman wore to the Oscars ceremony a couple of years ago? If the red carpets invites are thin on the ground for you, invest in striking silver or pearl jewellery instead; it's the easiest way to wear these colours. Alternatively tap into your inner goddess with a soft shell-pink wrap and mother-of-pearl make up – great against a tan. Light colours close to your face can reflect light, and take years off you too.

- Don't be afraid of hipster jeans. They may seem the preserve of nubile girly band members but they can be really flattering whatever your age as they create the illusion of having smaller hips. Just keep a close eye on the flesh overhang because it can ruin the effect. Stick if possible to the boot leg cut – it's even more flattering since it makes your legs look longer and slimmer.

- Always wear a heel, however slight. Even tall women can get away with tiny tapering heels. The extra inch or two will add length and can make you more aware of your posture.

■ Stick to textured fabrics. They can help to 'break up' flesh. Think linen, wool or even crinkled man-made fabrics.

■ Disguise a big bust with V-necks and low scoop necks. Avoid slash necks and halter necks altogether as they just make you look bulky.

■ Always choose trousers with hems long enough to skim the tip of a boot or shoe. They may feel too long, but they'll immediately draw the eye down, giving the impression of a longer, leaner leg. And avoid tapered trousers or clam diggers or pedal pushers for the same reason – they make almost everyone's legs look shorter and squatter, and thighs look bigger than they are.

■ Investing in good lingerie can knock pounds off you; go for well fitting bras with uplift and knickers that flatten in the right places. With bras, aim to banish seams, puckering and surplus flesh bursting out of cups (unless it's what you're aiming for).

24. Dressing yourself slim – men

Time to lose weight. While you know a good diet and exercise are the real answers, you'd actually like to look lighter right here, right now. Here's how to make the Fat Boy look Slim.

Defining idea...

'He who does not mind his belly will hardly mind anything else.'
SAMUEL JOHNSON

Time to fess up: it was you that ate all the pies. As if you were ever kidding anyone in those baggy tracksuit trousers and oversized sweatshirts. Just as Mr Comb-Over is the only person in the world who thinks his hairstyle is hiding rather than accentuating his baldness, Mr Huge Baggy-Clothing is not camouflaging the wobbly bits, as he hopes, but rather labelling himself straight off as Lardy Arse Love Handle Man. So stop it right now. Women have known for years how to make themselves look slimmer just by what they slip on, now it's our turn. We both know that there's nothing wrong with your body; there's just a little more to love than there used to be. Even so, there's no need to show the world that.

For a start you want to lose the baggy and don't even think about the tight. Baggy clothing may make you feel more comfortably camouflaged but the very nature of loose clothing means it will only make your spare tyre seem larger and more flabby than ever. As for tight clothing you'd think that would be obvious but you'll still see blokes in trousers that are too small for them. This seems to work on the basis that if you can pull the belt in tighter you can make the gut go away. Sadly fat, like breeding, is one of those things that will out and if you squeeze it in the middle it will look for another exit, often creating the phenomenon of two guts, one above the belt, one just above the crutch (mmm, very Brad Pitt). Quite simply, you need to make sure that clothes fit perfectly. Don't trust your own judgement on this, not least since you can't see all of yourself at once. It's a sad feature of being male that our bodies are always out to surprise us. Not only do we lose hair where we want it and gain it in unimaginable places, but just because you've got the gut in your sights that doesn't stop a bit of podge popping out where you can't see it – the crease under your arm for example. So take a friend (not too good a friend, and preferably female) when you buy clothes and do the full twirl for them to let them decide when you've found the kindest cut.

Here's an idea for you...

Since it's your waistline that's the problem in the first place, why draw attention to it? Big shiny belt buckles are a no-no. If you're wearing jackets try wearing braces because the belt itself is one of the things that catches the eye. Take that mobile phone out of your trouser pockets and put the wallet in a jacket pocket – the last thing you want is to add unsightly lumps to your profile. Make sure your trouser legs are long enough to cover up your socks and continue the long elegant line of your body (ahem). Gorblimey trousers that don't reach the end of your legs don't make your legs look longer, they just make your lower half look dumpier and wider.

The debate about double breasted and single breasted jackets rages on as ever but the general feeling is that they should be long enough to hang below your bum (yes it does look big in that) and that a well-cut double breasted jacket is far better for making your torso look longer and slimmer. It's all part of the oldest optical trick in the book, which is that horizontal lines make you look wider (so bin the hooped rugby shirt) and vertical lines make you seem longer and loftier (cue the pin stripes).

Similarly, if you're a little vertically challenged, try to avoid cardigans and jackets with more than three buttons because they are intended for the long of torso and will often make you look dumpier. Matching the tops and the trousers in terms of colour and design will help them blend into each other and help visually lengthen the whole outfit. Female fashion writers insist that dark colours are more slimming so make a start with black and charcoal.

Oddly enough, platform heels probably won't help because they suggest you're self-conscious about your height. You might want to think about 'lifts' instead which slot into your shoes and add a more subtle bit of height.

25. Going global without leaving your bedroom

Offices in Bangkok, Beijing and Bognor! Even if you're a one-man band you can seemingly operate with international business addresses if you know how.

Defining idea...

'You have to have a global attitude.'
RUPERT MURDOCH

Maybe you need to be able to show an international network of offices, or a more prestigious address. Perhaps you're trying to appeal to customers in Poland and want to give them a local phone number to call. Or it could just be that you travel a lot and want your old mum to have a single local number she can call at local rates and still get hold of you. All this is possible if you know how.

Would you like to have a Hollywood address? Would your business card be that much more compelling with phone and fax numbers for Japan, the US or Paris? What about a local phone number for friends to call that will ring where you are, wherever you are in the world? Thinking globally and acting locally isn't just a catchphrase for big business, it's just as possible for the little guy.

Postal addresses

Being able to receive mail somewhere else has always been relatively easy – that's what PO boxes are for. The problem is that everybody knows what a PO box is and having a phone number for that address makes it clear that you don't really have a home or office there – exactly the opposite of the impression you wanted to make. What you need instead is an international mail drop service. Mail Service Center (www.mailservicecenter.com) in the US, for example, will give you a prestigious LA or Hollywood address, and then quietly forward your mail back home to Dead Dog, Arkansas, or wherever it is you really live. British Monomarks (www.britishmonomarks.co.uk) will do the same for London, and Continental Relay (www.continentalrelay.com) will cheerily line you up with addresses and phone numbers in the US, Australia, and the UK all in one go. They can all be set up online so there's no need to leave home to acquire your new jet set image. You will be charged differently depending on where they have to send your mail, and packages will push the price up so shop around.

Fax and phone

Getting a foreign fax or phone number has never been easier and you can have the options of having someone else answer for you, having voicemail that's forwarded to you, or having your phone/computer take the call live on the other side of the planet. Right now it's possible to pick your own local fax and voicemail number all over the world. One company, J2, offers over 1,300 cities. Faxes sent to that number can be automatically converted to emails and sent to your mobile phone or email account.

Voice calls have been revolutionised by Internet Technology via a technology called Voice over Internet Protocol (VoIP, in geekspeak). Basically what that means is that you speak into a microphone (which can be a call-centre style headset or be just like a normal phone) attached to a computer. It digitises your voice and sends it over the Internet like a high-speed email. Now that Internet connections are usually flat fee for unlimited time, that effectively means unlimited free phoning, anywhere in the world. This means you can have a 'number' in New York that is really a computer that digitises the call and zips it down the lines to your bedroom in old York.

Here's an idea for you...

You've heard the hype, now try the Skype. Skype is a computer-based telephony program that runs on pretty much any computer and for the cost of a microphone headset turns your computer into a phone. Calling other Skype users, anywhere in the world, is free but you can also make calls to traditional phones at low rates or pay for a SkypeIn local number. If you have a SkypeIn number in, say, Poland, anyone in Poland can call it for a local rate while you receive the calls instantly wherever you may happen to be. The cost of a SkypeIn number, currently available in ten or so countries, is only 30 euros a year, which makes it worth while if you're often on the move but only want to hand out one number.

Numerous companies now offer VoIP services so that you can answer your phone to customers or friends calling a foreign number. However, quality of service and prices do vary so ask if you can have a trial before committing yourself to a long-term contract.

26. Cheat's cuisine: how to host without skill or effort

Special occasion looming? Naturally, the smart move would be to serve up a cordon bleu foodgasm but (a) you haven't got the ability and (b) you can't be arsed. Time to cheat.

Defining idea...

'Cooking is like love. It should be entered into with abandon or not at all.'

HARRIET VAN HORNE, US author. (All very well for her to say but some of us have ulterior motives to worry about.)

So you eat ready meals – who doesn't? Except that this time you've got someone coming round for dinner, or it's a romantic occasion, or there's a growing feeling that you're just a loafer in the home. Fraudulent cooking is one of the finest arts for the aspiring cad or caddess to master (mistress?). Skill with food conveys an air of worldliness, an understanding of the finer things in life, a practical ability in the kitchen and it can get you out of all kinds of scrapes by suggesting simultaneously that you are pulling your weight in the household and of course you love him/her.

The bottom line is that you are going to go out and get that supermarket ready meal because it's cheap and easy and even you know how to heat up lasagne. It's where you go from here that decides whether you are going to be hero or zero come suppertime.

Presentation is everything. Slap your pasta down on the table in its tinfoil package and you might as well pack your bags. Instead make a big fuss of needing to be left alone in the kitchen (this is why chefs develop their melodramatic flair) so no one can see what you're up to and remember to dispose of the wrappings very carefully indeed. The rest of the devilry is in the detail.

Lay the table with side plates for bread and butter. Have the butter itself in a ramekin (those little white bowls you always thought were ashtrays) and remember to lay out separate (larger) glasses for water as well as those for wine. Remember the candle – not only

Here's an idea for you...

Check online for gourmet delivery companies that deliver the ingredients and instructions. Leaping Salmon blazed this particular trail by delivering top-quality ingredients to culinarily challenged Londoners. The meals come in kits, already washed, sliced and measured, just waiting for you to throw together, heat according to instructions and then emerge triumphantly to general applause (as long as you remember to hide the instructions afterwards). The idea has caught on and similar outfits are offering the meal kit approaches at mainline stations and on the Internet. Don't forget that all the above tips are still applicable, even if you've craftily ordered out.

does it look romantic but it hides a multitude of sins when it comes to your food. Big white plates always work best and all food that's brought to the table should be in a serving dish (the plastic microwave tub doesn't count).

Garnishes are by far the easiest way of making dull grub look like haute cuisine. Fresh herbs are the best and the Getting Away With It team's favourite recommendation is Delia Smith's tip of throwing a handful of fresh Basil leaves over any pasta dish – tastes great, looks pro.

If you're really pushing the boat out and trying to make up for major misdemeanours then get hold of some edible flowers for a garnish. Cheese shavings (reach for the vegetable peeler) or ground nuts also work wonders. A swirl of cream (or yoghurt if weight conscious) will transform even tinned soups, stews, and curries, especially if you then dust it with a bit of ground paprika. Judiciously placed olives will do the same for hummus, tsatsiki, and pretty much any other dip. If you're going to have good old veg, then remember that baby versions of the corn, carrots, cabbages et al. not only look exotic and cute but also cook faster (result!).

A few easy touches can transform the simplest of things. Shop-bought meals are usually quickly recognised so go for the fancy premium versions available from the more up-market supermarkets and then slice mozzarella on top, melt it and garnish with fresh herbs so it looks different. A baguette or piece of pitta is bread but slice it diagonally, toast it and pour a little olive oil on it and it becomes cold-pressed, drizzled crostini. You didn't know you had it in you, did you?

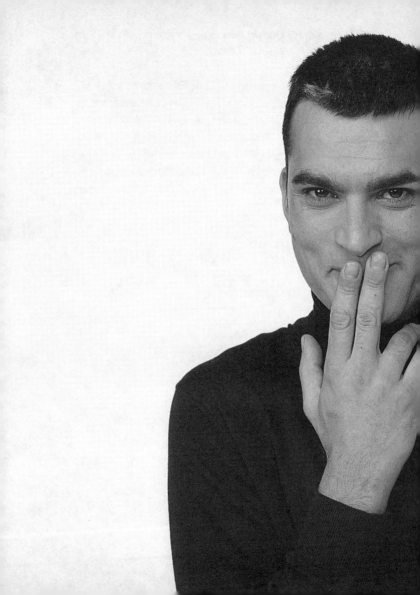

Rescuing a bad situation

27. Lying – and not being caught

Lying isn't always a bad thing – we're all familiar with white lies, with business bluffing, and protecting people's feelings. As long as we don't get found out, no problem.

Defining idea...

'No high-minded man, no man of right feeling, can contemplate the lumbering and slovenly lying of the present day without grieving to see a noble art so prostituted.'
MARK TWAIN on the art of lying.

We at the Getting Away With It team are confident that you only have other people's best interests at heart when you want to deceive and thrive. Instead of guilt, all we need concern ourselves with is not being rumbled. Bad liars get caught for a number of reasons but the most likely are: failing to deliver the lie convincingly; failing to do the necessary homework; and failing to prepare a fallback lie.

Failing to lie convincingly is a beginner's mistake and suggests that the liar is either totally unprepared, very nervous or cursed with a conscience like a plague of Jiminy Crickets. You'll have noticed that some people lie naturally and easily – otherwise we wouldn't have lawyers and politicians. The trick – as it so often is in getting away with things – is confidence. At the pathological end of the scale, these liars are utterly convincing because they actually believe their own lies.

To be convincing there are a couple of musts. Firstly, never be forced into telling a lie off the top of your head: practise it over and over so that it comes out perfectly naturally. Then rationalise it until it seems reasonable – you'd be surprised how even the utterly implausible can be made to sound reasonable if you try hard enough. If you're likely to be asked about having sex with the post boy, question for yourself whether anything other than full sex with a view to reproduction really counts. Do this often enough and you too will be able to deny with a straight face that you had sex with someone even though you regularly fornicated like ferrets in a sack. (This won't work if that person has clothing stained with your bodily fluids by the way.)

Do your homework because a good lie is a simple lie, and the common everyday lie is often made more convincing by being decked out with some concrete details. Don't say you were in the pub with mates. Say you were in the Rat and Drainpipe with Bill and Ted. It's just that much more precise for the listener and so paints a more realistic scene. (The exception to this is that there are some things we never remember, so a policeman who asks what you were doing at 9.00 p.m. on Wednesday three years ago will know for sure you're lying if you come snapping back with names and locations.)

Obviously there's no point delivering detail if it is going to melt away like mist as soon as the light of investigation is shone on it. Try to come up with details that can't be checked or, if they can, make sure they do tally. Try not to bring other people into the loop – asking Bill and Ted to provide an alibi for something is a highly risky strategy and greatly increases the chance of the lie being rumbled. Not just because Bill and Ted are themselves rubbish liars, but simply because with more than one person trotting out a made-up story inconsistencies are sure to start appearing.

This point is why you need to prepare a 'follow-up lie' (FUL). The FUL is kept in reserve for when your original porky pie is crumbling in front of your face. This requires good acting ability so you will need your FUL to be even better rehearsed than the original. A FUL requires careful delivery. It must be seen to be dragged physically from you, with all the pain and messiness of pulling teeth. Above all it must be cringingly embarrassing – which will immediately explain why you

Here's an idea for you...

Before you try it on other people, always practise telling your lie in front of a mirror. Watch your body language. Give-aways include raising your hands to your mouth, any nervous foot tapping or movements, folding your arms around your body, and confused gestures like shrugging as you say 'yes'. Practise the lie until your body shows no stress when you tell it. Say it often enough and you might even start to believe it wholeheartedly, at which point you are ready for the telling (and for launching yourself into politics). To spot your weaknesses, practise a couple of totally random lies right now – you could start with something utterly implausible like 'I never inhaled' or 'this war is not about oil'.

told the first lie. If, for example, your FUL is that you were seeing the doc about a really foul personal hygiene problem you will have explained lie one, discouraged further questions, and possibly gained sympathy all in one go. Result!

28. Getting hog-whimperingly drunk without the hangover

The morning after. The words alone have us reaching for coffee and shades. What on earth can we do to dodge that hell? Well, just find the time it takes to read this idea.

Defining idea...

'He resolved, having done it once, never to move his eyeballs again.'
KINGSLEY AMIS

Booze: it's not big and it's not clever. It shrivels your liver, puts pounds on your paunch and hoovers the content of your wallet. Worst of all, it leads to the inevitable revelation, usually around two in the morning, that you – yes, you – are in fact the greatest dancer in the world and you don't care who knows it. Then, before you know it, the next day dawns and you've got a pounding head, bleary eyes, and that yummy baboon's armpit sort of feeling in the mouth. Frankly, if that's all you wake up with, you can consider yourself lucky. But wouldn't it be nice if it didn't have to be that way?

The obvious way of dodging hangovers would be not to get drunk, but if you wanted that kind of advice you could have asked your mum for it. There are alternatives.

Before you get drunk
The old college-boy stories about lining your stomach with milk are partly right. It's not that you can literally 'line' your stomach; it's the simple fact that your body will process the alcohol more steadily if it's absorbed along with food, so eat before your jiggle-juice bonanza.

Choose your poison
'Gin makes you sin', 'whisky makes you frisky', 'beer before wine, you'll feel fine' – lyrical verse, doubtless, but entirely fact free. What matters is clarity, purity and quality. The active ingredient in booze is ethanol, a natty little substance, part drug, part food, which your body happily gets to work on to transform so as to metabolise the sugars. So far, so good, except that en route there is a by-product called acetaldehyde: this is vile stuff and is largely responsible for the next-day nasties.

As ethanol goes stale it produces more acetaldehyde, so drinking last week's opened bottle of wine is a bad idea (tip – try finishing it off in one go first time around). The same applies to wines or mixes which are in the process of being distilled or fortified into something stronger. This means cheaper hooch made from low-quality ingredients is likely to pack a sucker punch. Avoid dodgy rum, sherry, et al. if you want to avoid the hangover from hell. And don't even think about 'shooters', in which the colour and sugar drown out any point in using good ingredients.

The other quotient is the congener count. Congeners occur naturally in fermented and distilled drinks and have been identified as another something that increases the hangover factor. Helpfully, the congener count comes with a rule of thumb that even the deeply bladdered can remember – the darker the drink, the higher the hangover risk. Thus port is one of the highest on the congener scale, vodka one of the lowest. It's not, strictly speaking, a congener factor, but drink anything green or blue and you're asking for it.

Here's an idea for you...

The jury's still out, but pills alternately known as RU-21 and KGB can be bought at a pharmacy to combat hangovers. Forget stories that the KGB developed them to help agents win drinking competitions – you're still going to get wasted, but the idea is that they speed up the breakdown of the acetaldehyde. The catch is you have to remember to take the pills when you're plastered, including before 'the last drink' (there's a last one!?), which in practice makes them less than reliable.

Remember this isn't the only factor – a poor-quality vodka can easily make up for its low congener count with an extra helping of acetaldehyde. That's the reason why you sometimes hear the boast that such and such booze can be drunk without risk. A product called Bismark schnapps seemed to be a likely contender but, in the end, the Getting Away With It team found that disproving such claims was just a matter of downing enough of the damn stuff.

During the drinking
Avoid carbonated mixers: fizzy drinks get you smashed faster, and that affects your drinking decisions (hmmm, a single malt, or one of everything in the optics?). Above all drink water – as much of it as you can before going to bed. Don't take headache pills in advance as this will put an extra strain on your liver and your liver don't love you no more as it is.

Next day
Ginger is great for settling the guts – try juicing some with apple. Water is good but an isotonic sports drink will get to your cells even better. Vitamins and minerals are also called for. NO, having a hair of the dog isn't a good idea and points the way down a slippery slope.

29. Making her happy ... after not-so-great sex

If you've just had sex and it was a bit of a flop, don't panic; there's still time to rescue the situation and have her purring for more.

If you can get away from the myth of genital sex being the most crucial part of a sexual encounter, there are endless ways to please your partner.

Defining idea...

'And so there we have it, the play process: foreplay, coreplay, and moreplay – taken as a whole, the makings of great sexual drama.'
DR IAN KERNER

Some men approach sexual intimacy like porno stars constantly seeking good 'wood'. They worry about how hard they are and how long they can last, but in reality only around 30% of women actually climax as a result of penetrative sex. That leaves plenty of room for sexual play where you're only limited by your imagination.

If you came a little quickly and she's still excited, instead of worrying about your performance, concentrate on getting her to climax. Ask her what feels good, or if she's shy, get her to push your head/hand/sex toy in the right direction. One of the easiest things to do is to slide down and play with her throbbing vagina and clitoris with your lips or fingers. The feel of a soft tongue on her already sensitised clitoris and vulva can feel especially good after she's already been penetrated. Dr Ian Kerner suggests in *She Comes First: The Thinking Man's Guide to Pleasuring a Woman* that oral sex, rather than being an optional element of foreplay, is actually 'coreplay' and that men can become better lovers simply by giving more oral sex.

Rather than diving straight into action, try teasing her first by licking her legs, thighs and belly so she'll be more excited when you actually get down to business. Get her to put her hand on your head and to guide you to the right spot. Some women prefer clitoral stimulation, but others have more sensation on the labia lips, or just inside the vagina. Let her guide you with her hands or voice. Cunnilingus is an art in itself and there are many variations of tongue movements. You can try moving your tongue in small circles, clockwise or anticlockwise, up and down, from left to right as well as varying the speed. Some women like the sensation of your lips on their vaginas as well as your tongue. Experiment with different

Here's an idea for you...

If you feel unsure about how to skilfully manipulate her clitoris and vulva area, try anal play instead. As well as being more straightforward, pleasuring an alternative erogenous zone can accentuate stimulation elsewhere. You can try massaging the anus with your fingers and/or tongue. If she likes it you'll soon find out! If you are not fluid-bonded you can use a dental dam over the area. She may prefer you to concentrate just on her anus, or tease her there in combination with vaginal stimulation. Go for it!

techniques, paying attention to her physical responses and
encourage her to indicate her preferences.

Some women find cunnilingus more stimulating in different
positions. For instance, doggy style is a great way to receive oral sex
because the vagina is naturally more open. Improve the missionary
position by putting a few pillows under her buttocks. When you
raise the area you also increase blood flow. You can also try kneeling
down at the foot of the bed/sofa/chair – often it's easier to practise
cunnilingus when you approach her genitals from a lower position.

If she likes penetration and finds it easier to climax this way, then
don't be afraid to use sex toys. The advantage of these is that you
can buy the shape/size/material that works best for her. Sex toy
play doesn't have to be about penetration, it could be that just the
thrill of a buzzing vibrator or a partial insertion of a dildo is
enough. Use lube with sex toys and be gentle at first, when she
wants it plunged in to the hilt, she'll let you know.

If you have a shy partner, get her to sit on your lap with her back
to you and encourage her to play with herself while you massage
her legs and breasts. This position should reassure her enough to
be able to let go and climax.

Finally, don't forget after-play, the caressing and touching that
makes the come-down just as good as going up.

30. Of course I didn't forget, darling

Do not be fooled into thinking that perfect performance during the other 99.7% of the year can help you if you forget that one special day and you don't know how to get away with it.

Defining idea...

'If it weren't for marriage, men and women would have to fight with total strangers.'
DAVE BARRY, American humourist

There are three important days in the Official Relationship Calendar: your partner's birthday, your anniversary and Valentine's Day. Should be easy to remember, huh? But we know it's not.

Alert readers will have already gathered that this is really a guy chapter. If you're not a guy, you might prefer to skip on to the next idea, because you don't really want to know about the things we're covering here. Or, more accurately, you do want to know, but please, it's better for the males among us if you don't.

Valentine's Day
St. Valentine himself wouldn't associate this day with happy thoughts. Having been arrested for illegally marrying couples during the reign of Roman Emperor Claudius II, on 14 February he

was beaten to death with clubs and his head was cut off and put on a spike. Those of us who have forgotten St. Valentine's Day will know how he must have felt.

If you somehow miss the prompts that 14 February is approaching – for example, by spending the first six weeks of the year in a remote cave – the sudden realisation that you are expected to be calculatedly romantic for the day can be a nasty shock. The first five minutes of this crisis are the most important. Never admit you have forgotten. Use a raised eyebrow and cheeky grin to suggest that you have something huge planned meticulously for later in the day. If you have failed to convince, attempt some light-hearted tickling or banter to show how relaxed and carefree you are.

Only a very naïve partner will fall for this completely. It's a stalling tactic so you can get to the office, where you can't be watched like a hawk while you fix the problem. This involves the application of money in liberal doses. Your first call is always to the florist closest to her location, the one who will deliver a bunch of flowers for a delivery fee nudging three figures. Forget non-local florists. They don't need your kind of business today, and won't deliver until several days after your relationship has been terminated.

No matter how desperate you are, never, ever, buy flowers from a garage.

When booking a restaurant, don't start with the lovely little brasserie around the corner. It was booked solid eight months ago. You're going to have to aim for restaurants that you can't afford, because people like you who aren't idiots have booked all the affordable ones. Remember, you have set up the expectation that you have everything planned, so a tandoori 50 miles away is not good enough. Never go out without a reservation: four freezing hours of fruitlessly touring restaurants packed with smug couples is not a romantic date.

Anniversaries

Your anniversary is easier to plan at one hour's notice: unlike Valentine's Day, the rest of the male population isn't frantically doing the same thing as you are. However, anniversaries involve the vague expectation that you will do something romantic and intimate that doesn't involve underwear until much later. This can be confusing and stressful.

Here's an idea for you...

Go for a high-risk, high-reward scenario: cook something. To do this, you have to be able to use the cooker, so look at the instruction manual, and the meal has to be something that your partner actually likes, so try and remember what that is. Buy the book by the chef that she likes watching on TV, and pick something with not many ingredients that takes less than four hours. The beauty of cooking is that, short of actually poisoning your loved one, you're allowed to make mistakes. At least one component might well be inedible, but that's endearing. Start cooking before she arrives home. Wear an apron. Light a candle. These items are readily available from many shops. Put on that CD of hers that she knows you hate.

Birthdays

The most important thing when forgetting your partner's birthday is to realise you've forgotten on the day. There are some early clues to warn you that you may have forgotten: you will probably experience a moody silence; there will be lots of brightly coloured envelopes that are not addressed to you in the morning post; her relatives will call and sing happy birthday down the phone.

When the penny drops, act with speed and efficiency. For this, forward planning is the essence. You can start planning right now for the inevitable day when this happens to you. Keep an emergency greetings card in the house. When she said, 'I'd really like one of those for a present,' six months ago while you were watching TV or reading the Sunday colour supplement, you did write down what she was referring to, didn't you? Giving her something that has previously been mentioned in an offhand way (because that's why she brought it up) shows you have been planning this for months, and couldn't really have forgotten her birthday. Accept her apology with good grace, and immediately start the preparation for when you forget again next year. The key to long-term success is not to overestimate your ability to learn from experience.

31. Jumping job when you've been rumbled

Here's how to get another job with a fat-cat salary when in your current job you've done nothing, nada, nix, not a sausage, and until now you've got away with it.

Defining idea...

'One of the symptoms of approaching nervous breakdown is the belief that one's work is important.'
BERTRAND RUSSELL

You've got away with it for two years. You're a legend at work; people talk about your continuous inactivity with awe. You've bumped up your 'working at home' days to two and a half a week and you've got a team that covers for you. But, you've been sussed. Your boss has discovered, or more likely been briefed, that you are what you actually are – a complete waste of space. It's time to move on.

We need to make another assumption here: it's much easier to move on in the same organisation than a new one. Where you are, you already know the levers to pull and the buttons to press to avoid work and, more importantly, avoid trouble. It's just not the time to relearn all of that in another place. No, you've got to move on in the same organisation. But you've got to get a new job against a background that the boss you've got right now thinks you're a skiver. And as sure as eggs are eggs, any potential new manager will ask your current boss for his or her opinion of you. However, this is much less of a problem than it seems.

It may surprise you, but your biggest allies in this enforced change of job are the people in the human resources department. 'But', we hear you gasp, 'they're the people who measure productivity, who check progress against objectives and generally are trained to spot skill gaps and non-jobs.' Correct, but they're also the people who make absolutely sure that managers adhere rigidly to dismissal and other personnel processes. That's why they're your best friends right now. Firing someone is very hard work and no managers want to go through the whole bureaucratic rigmarole if they don't have to, and that includes your boss. Think about it from your boss's point of view. The personnel department will dig for evidence. They'll find and brandish your last appraisal where the person who's trying to fire you said such nice things about you and your dedication to the organisation and hard work. They'll make your boss fill in forms, make statements and struggle through a long series of verbal warnings, written warnings, having witnesses at the meetings, offering you the chance to have a witness at the meetings and so forth. No one wants to do this; it's like swimming in treacle or kicking a sponge. Most people will do anything not to have to do it.

You need a reference

OK, you've searched the house magazine and found a new job that's suitable. It's a bit more money (nobody believes that anyone voluntarily moves sideways) but it's not so much that it would make your old boss jealous or even hopping mad. You've gone to the interviews and knocked their socks off. There's only one small cloud on the horizon – the new people are bound to talk to your boss. Answer: get your retaliation in first.

Talk to your boss. You have two objectives. First, help him or her to understand that you're not likely to give up easily if they try to sink you. Make it quite clear that you're not going to go quietly. This one is going to end in court and they're going to have to explain to a lot of people why they didn't realise that you've done absolutely bugger all for two whole years. Now find some positives. Why is the new job more suitable for your talents? Give them ammunition to fire that makes them enthusiastic about your ability and willingness to do the new job without saying anything at all about how you've done the old one. Remember: they're only looking for reasons to advance your case; they've already decided to avoid the pain of sacking you.

Here's an idea for you...

Never treat an appraisal as an ego-trip. An appraisal is an important document to be used in evidence as you pursue your route to the top without actually doing anything. Think about the wording with the HR department in mind. All you need is to make sure it says that you've done what you were expected to do and that you're a loyal servant of the organisation. Those are the two things an employment tribunal are looking for.

Think about this reference business before you choose your new manager. Anyone your boss hates is a good candidate. 'Not only have I got rid of Ken, but he's gone to Roger. That should slow him down a bit.' Anyone your boss doesn't know can also be the right person: 'Well, it's no skin off my nose'.

32. Complain and prosper

We can all complain but there's a big difference between letting off steam and focused complaining with a view to coming away with something beneficial. Complain to gain.

An American friend of the Getting Away With It team once contemplated setting up a complaints agency in London because she was appalled at how ineffectively the Brits complain. In a country where 'mustn't grumble' is a maxim to live by, this ineptitude is probably to be expected.

Accepting bad service or a poor product is like announcing you're not worth being treated properly, so don't. Equally, however, the smarter complainer knows that complaining is about much more than just getting a gripe off your chest. Some people have a knack

Defining idea...

'I think a compliment ought to always precede a complaint, where one is possible, because it softens resentment and insures for the complaint a courteous and gentle reception.'
MARK TWAIN

of turning bad situations to their advantage. One lady who caught her foot in a faulty swing door ended up being given the money for a week's holiday. Go in there knowing exactly what you're doing and with a bit of luck you'll walk away with a lot more than a bit of guilty satisfaction at having chewed out some miserable wage slave.

First off, don't get angry; get even, or better. Keep your composure at all times and if you feel like you're about to boil over then walk away and complain when you're cooler. A firm, not furious, line is far more likely to get you somewhere.

Be clear about what you want to get from the complaint. Take the time to think about what you consider adequate compensation, whether that is money, product replacement or some kind of reward. Offer your solution to the company. If they realise you're not going to go away then they may even accept it there and then.

Follow the paper trail. Take notes. Keep all documentation and if you can record conversations and phone calls, then do so. You have to tell people you're recording them but that works in your favour since it shows that you are taking this very seriously and you're likely to be the kind of industrial strength pain in the arse that doesn't go away. It also suggests you may be thinking of going down the legal path, and they won't want that.

It's not personal. You won't get anywhere if you turn this into a shouting match. Get the name of the person you're talking to but make it clear you know it's not them, but the company/service /product that you are complaining about. If it is the person that's upset you then you should be complaining to someone else anyway.

Complain to someone else. In fact complain to everyone. Not just the person in front of you but their boss, their customer service department and their mum if you can find the phone number. The more places you fire your complaint off to, the more likely it is that it will be replied to. Be careful in escalating, though. Demanding to see a supervisor is never as effective as saying 'I know it's not your fault and I don't see why you should have to deal with this aggro so why don't you pass me on to a supervisor – that's why they get paid more than you'. You never know when the person in front of you may even turn out to be an ally.

Here's an idea for you...

No good actor would show up without having read the script and a successful complainer is every bit as much a player. So script your complaint carefully before you get stuck in. If you're at all unsure, get help from a better wordsmith or complainer. Writing it all down helps focus on what exactly you were unhappy with, and just what you expect to see done about it. It also means you will be deadly in your consistency and if you end up dealing with many managers and call centres it makes your life so much easier.

Don't stop complaining. Your nightmare is being passed to a call centre that handles complaints but if you can't help but do that remember everyone in a call centre is under pressure to end each call within a certain time. Repeat yourself over and over making it clear that you can and will do this all day unless you get an acceptable answer.

33. Clawing your way back from fatal faux pas

There are many books about etiquette and how to avoid social gaffes written by people who are skilled in the subject. These books are not for you.

Defining idea...

'The path of social advancement is, and must be, strewn with broken friendships.'
H. G. WELLS

The problem with etiquette books is that they don't take account of the environmental factors involved. The people that write them have long ago achieved power over their own destiny and manners, while you have not. This is a fancy way to say that you're often drunk, trying to get drunk, or thinking that the only way to get through the following three-hour social situation is to get even more drunk.

This is a disadvantage. Your short- and long-term memory is impaired by the effects of alcohol, as is your judgement of situations. In combination, the two factors can have awkward consequences – such as simultaneously having sex with someone and forgetting his or her name. In case you were wondering, this example is a serious gaffe, especially if the person is a relative, a relative of your spouse, or the guy who came to install satellite TV.

All of the techniques below can be performed drunk. In fact, that's the only time most people could get away with any of them. The key is total commitment. Don't worry about practice: trust us, you'll get plenty of that.

The maiden aunt: This is strictly for when you have more social status than the person you are talking to. It has the advantage of honesty and can be used for any gaffe. It has the disadvantage that you will regularly cause offence, but if you've bought this book, that ship has probably sailed already. You stop talking, stare at the person as if they have just arrived on the planet at that moment and then say, loudly and firmly, 'You know, I've completely forgotten who you are' or 'I think that was your girlfriend I just goosed'. There is a limit on the number of times you use this on the same person.

The designated driver: Travel everywhere with a friend who is more charming and responsible than you. When you insult or offend someone, your chaperone is on hand to clear up the mess. This is an approach favoured by upper class British males, among whom it is known as 'marriage'.

The bon vivant: This one has the advantage that it can be used repeatedly throughout an evening. Whenever two people approach whose names and personal details you can't for the life of you remember, grab them warmly and shout 'My guys! Now I'm sure you two must have met before!' Do this confidently enough, and they will bask in your approval. You can thereafter say or do more or less what you like, because you are The Man. Take care that they aren't already good friends, or they may turn round and say, 'Yes, but who are you?' In which case, use the Cleese (see below).

Here's an idea for you...

To avoid forgotten name embarrassment, use the 'buy one, get one free' tactic. You're standing with a good friend or partner (let's call him Derek) and someone whose name you have forgotten approaches. Make a one-sided introduction. 'Hi! Great to see you again!' you say to the stranger, who is either your boss or the guy who collects the pint glasses – you can't quite remember – 'This is Derek!' Hopefully, the boss/glass collector will give his or her name without a prompt. If not, you're stuffed.

The Cleese: A panic measure, to be used only in extreme situations. Elaborately feign a distraction. This may involve attending to an untied shoelace (if possible, your own) or pretending to choke on a cocktail sausage. Fainting is usually too extreme and potentially hazardous.

The woolly: This is often employed in a family situation. For example, when you have children, you are so tired you can barely remember their names, never mind the names of all the babies that belong to the people who used to be your friends. Your friends, however, consider their children's names to be somewhat important, and would be offended if they knew you had forgotten. So on emails, cards and letters, use general forms of greeting if in doubt. 'The Smith family' is slightly formal. 'Ian and Deb and family' is better, but remember, if they only have one child, you've just given the game away. Using 'How are the little ones?' normally gets a response that 'Jemima is extraordinary, she's reading already, and Jason still has that twitch.' Forget the dull anecdotes (you'll hear them again), just write down the names. If you think this isn't true, just wait until Christmas and see how many of your cards are addressed to 'All at number 42'. They're all doing it.

34. Getting away with murder

Getting away with murder is, thankfully, not easy. Although we don't want to make it any easier, there are a few things that history shows us it's best not to do.

Don't repeat a winning formula

George Joseph Smith devised an excellent murder method, all the better because he actually obtained the unwitting collusion of his victims. Smith met and married susceptible young ladies with attractive bank balances. He was able, with his solicitous charm, to persuade them that they had had fainting fits, and so the unsuspecting girl would go to her doctor for help. Days later she would be found drowned in her bath. This worked very well three times. However, the newspapers carried accounts of the third bride's tragic fate, and these were read by the father of bride number two, who alerted the police. Smith was hanged in August 1915.

Don't confess

Frederick Field had a splendid plan that worked once, but his stupidity in trying it again is almost incredible. In 1931, the strangled body of a prostitute was found in an empty building. Field, one of the workmen who found the body, claimed he had given the key to another man but he was proved to have been lying. In July 1933, Field called at a newspaper office and confessed to the murder, bargaining that the defence costs would be paid by the press. He retracted his confession at the trial. It was clear that the confession was a ploy to obtain money, and since his statement varied from the known facts, the judge directed the jury to acquit. In 1936, he was arrested as a deserter from the RAF. He at once confessed to another murder. Then, at the trial, he again retracted the confession. This time the jury took fifteen minutes to find him guilty, and he was hanged.

Don't anticipate

Struggling to cope with the costs of one child, Arthur Devereux was horrified when his wife Beatrice then gave birth to twins. Devereux persuaded his wife to drink poison and give some to the twins, telling her it was cough medicine. He placed the bodies in a trunk, and moved to a new address. Beatrice's mother, disturbed at her daughter's disappearance, was not to be put off by Arthur's excuses. She traced the trunk to a warehouse, and ordered it to be opened. Devereux's explanation was that his wife had killed herself and the twins, and that he had panicked and concealed the bodies. Could he have got away with it? We shall never know, because there was one other vital piece of evidence. Devereux had applied for a job before his wife's death, and on that application he had described himself as a widower. He was hanged in August 1905.

Do not write an account of your crime
In 1942, a woman was found murdered in Brompton Road, Strood, UK. Her son was able to tell the police his mother had been killed by a soldier. Gunner Reginald Buckfield was among those questioned and was found to be a deserter. He was handed over to the military authorities. No doubt his time in police custody was tedious so to while away the hours he decided to do some writing, penning a murder story entitled 'The Mystery of Brompton Road'. He claimed that the writing was pure fiction, but it revealed a direct knowledge of the facts of the crime. He was found guilty of murder and committed to Broadmoor.

Here's an idea for you...

Remember that the perfect crime isn't the one nobody knows about, but the one nobody can touch you for. In 1909, during Peary's eighth attempt to reach the North Pole, Professor Ross Marvin set off to explore with two Eskimos. When the Eskimos returned they reported that they had found Marvin drowned under a layer of ice. In 1926, the two approached a Danish missionary, who had been carrying out work among the Eskimos, and admitted that they had shot Marvin, saying that his cruel and hysterical behaviour had proved that he was 'ice-mad' and a danger. Fortunately for them, they had confessed to murder in a land over which there was no legal jurisdiction.

35. Dodge that parking ticket

Local authorities tell us that if we don't park illegally we won't get a ticket but the reality is not always so clear cut. Don't be had; appeal.

Defining idea...

'Politics is not worrying this country one-tenth as much as where to find a parking space.'
WILL ROGERS

Since the parking ticket business was privatized the rules of the game have changed, not least because the ticket issuers make money out of handing out more tickets, the result of which is that some of them are more than a little questionable. Don't forget that the people issuing the tickets are under great pressure to do so (at least one warden has been fired for not handing out enough) and so there is even less point in arguing the toss with them – not that arguing over a ticket was often very profitable in the old days. Instead take the matter up with their bosses by appealing the ticket with the local authority.

The number of tickets being handed out has trebled since privatization. According to Ticketbusters (www.ticketbusters.co.uk), over 5.8 million tickets were issued in London alone last year. Of those, Ticketbusters claim a stunning 60% were issued incorrectly and yet the number of appeals against tickets is astonishingly low.

Just 0.06% of tickets are appealed against in the Westminster borough yet over 60% of appeals are upheld.

To be fair, that high rate of upheld appeals probably reflects the fact that most people only appeal when they're on pretty solid ground. However, the flip side is that a huge number of us don't think of appealing; we just resign ourselves to coughing up – much to the delight of the ticket issuers (Westminster earned a staggering £100 million last year).

There are a few points to bear in mind if you come back to find your wheels are sporting fresh paperwork. The first is that if you pay up that's the end of it so if you think you have a chance of appealing then you shouldn't pay. Don't be put off by the cost scaling, whereby delaying makes the fine larger – this will usually be frozen if the ticket is being appealed so even if you lose the appeal you should still be charged as if you paid the fine immediately. This is also the one and only time when your council's bureaucratic inertia can work in your favour because if the local authority fails to reply to you within a set period (typically 56 days) of receiving your appeal then they are supposed to cancel it.

There are a number of common points that can be appealed against. Unfortunately there are also some 'pub wisdom' points that don't necessarily cut it. You may be told that the fine isn't applicable if the wardens weren't wearing their hats when they issued it. This is based on a half truth in that the law stipulates that they must be in uniform. Those in the business, however, say that this is unlikely to be a good enough reason on its own, although it could be a further factor in an appeal based on other grounds. You may also be told that there is a 'grace period' in which you can't be ticketed; five minutes or so to get change for the meter, that sort of thing. Sadly, this seems to be entirely at the discretion of the local authority, and so can't be counted on to get you off the hook.

What you can appeal for, however, are incorrect details on the ticket (how many people bother to read it all?), including the colour of the car. You can also appeal against your car being clamped even though you had returned to it before the padlock was clipped shut. Likewise, if you make it back to a vehicle being picked up by a crane before the wheels are off the ground you can usually appeal. Of course you don't want an appeal to be just your

Here's an idea for you...

There are plenty of services that will keep you up to date on your local area's restrictions. If you are regularly having parking headaches and suspect you are being unfairly penalised, then it's probably worth signing up with them given that the annual subscription is usually a fraction of today's ticket costs. Try Ticketbusters (www.ticketbusters.co.uk), which costs just £10 and gives you access to all the local information plus advice on appealing. Also take a look at www.parkingticket.co.uk for some great freebie information about the technicalities of ticketing.

word against theirs so if you aren't carrying a camera with you (which is becoming less likely now that they're built into mobile phones) then make sure you get the details of any witnesses.

Yellow lines are meant to have a 'T' bar marking their beginnings and ends unless they are terminated by a line marking a parking/delivery bay. If they just stop or fade then you may be able to appeal against that. In any case where there is physical evidence, make sure you record it yourself – for example, photographing the road markings or measuring street widths – because a well-prepared appeal is far more likely to succeed.

Getting rid of evidence

36. Stealth surfing

Your computer logs everything you do. When you're online, other computers are busy logging everywhere you go. If you'd rather surf in stealth, you must learn to become invisible.

Defining idea...

'Curiosity is lying in wait for every secret.'
RALPH WALDO EMERSON

Many people are surprised to learn that when we're on the Internet, we're never 100% anonymous – if the powers that be really want to find where you've been then they will. What you can do, though, is make it very hard indeed for family, friends and, perhaps most importantly, your employers to know where your tastes lie in the wonderful world of webbery. There are many levels on which you can be rumbled so let's start with the basic ones and move on up.

With your home/work machine you might think that closing down the browser means the end of your session but you'd be horrified what gets left behind. Internet browsers have a 'history' function which is basically a breadcrumb trail of everywhere you've been. Bad news. Bin it. The way to do that is to go to your browser and find the Tools menu. There you should find Options including both History (where you went) and Cache (files that have been stored to your hard disk while you were there) both of them being dead give-aways for where you've been and what you've been doing. Clear them both (with the 'clear' button) and set both to zero unless you want to leave a blatant record of what you're up to.

Don't bookmark a page you don't want others to find (you'd be surprised how many do). Check you didn't bookmark a page (for example, a chat room) in a previous existence when you had nothing to hide. While you're at it, ensure 'auto-complete' is off so that someone who accidentally starts typing another address or email address doesn't suddenly have the whole thing completed for them, exposing your secret penchants in the process.

Take the time to download some clean-up software such as *Perfect Privacy*, *Eraser*, *Complete Cleanup*, etc. There are many varieties of these, often free to try, which automatically wipe away the bits and bobs that filter down to your machine while you're online.

If that largely takes care of cleaning up your machine, there's always the issue of websites themselves knowing who you are and where you are coming from/going to. As far as the Net is concerned, you are (or rather your computer connection is) just a number but there are things at work out there (software trackers and marketing companies, for the main part) trying to join up the dots and identify us. At the very least, your Internet provider will know where you've been and if you access the web via a proxy server at work then so will your employer. To get around that you would need a cloak of invisibility. Fortunately they exist.

The usual approach is to surf via what's called an anonymous proxy. You don't go straight to the site you want; instead you go via a site which itself takes care of scrambling your identity so that the site can't see who you are. Of course the anonymous proxy could trace you if it had to (or if the police asked) but it's in their interest not to unless forced so that will usually hide you pretty well. The best known is Anonymizer (www.anonymizer.com) but there's a wide variety of alternative proxy servers and encryption solutions out there just waiting to turn you into the invisible man/woman.

A word of warning. If you're surfing from work and your employer is pretty paranoid then bear in mind that they may have keylogging software that records what everyone is doing and will spot your activity

Here's an idea for you...

One way of keeping your work machine as clean as possible is to use a USB memory key loaded with clean-up software and your own secure browser. When you want to wander the web, you ignore the browser installed on the machine and instead plug in the memory key and launch your own browser from there. There are numerous commercially available memory key/browser combos available with the beauty that while you use your work machine, you shouldn't end up leaving traces on it. Bear in mind, though, that even this will still be detected if the system has keylogging/spy software so find out what's watching you first.

even if unsure where you're going. There are anti-keylogging products, but the best thing is to ask a friend in the IT department what's in place and what it can and can't log.

For a useful list of tools that can hide you online try the Electronic Privacy Information Centre at www.epic.org/privacy/tools.html.

37. Disposing of a body

Like grouting tiles or landing a jumbo jet after the pilot is taken ill, disposing of a dead body is a skilled task that non-specialists (that's us) prefer not to perform. However, if needs must …

Defining idea…

'Dying is the most embarrassing thing that can ever happen to you, because someone's got to take care of all your details.'
ANDY WARHOL

If you are going to dispose of a dead body, ask yourself a few important questions. The first: how did you get stuck with this job? The second, and a question that will affect many of the decisions you will make, is what species are you disposing of? Hamster and goldfish burial, for example, is not as closely regulated as burying your friends and relatives. To be honest, you can stick a hamster in the nearest skip, so the decisions that need to be made focus on the well-being of the hamster's surviving owner. You can't get rid of the earthly remains of Uncle Al like this without risking police involvement. Nor can you use the same method as when you found Nemo floating on the top of his tank. Your toilet's just not big enough.

Let's deal with pets first. It's usual to want to bury your pet in your garden. Of the 1.5 million dogs and cats that die in the UK every year, 300,000 are buried at home. By all means, go ahead, unless you don't have a garden. If you do, 10 m from a stream and 1.5 m from underground pipes is the Environment Agency's regulation. And, please, 250 m from a water supply for human consumption. It's also bad form to bury your pet if you are moving out next month. If the new owners find the grave, it's likely to weird them out Stephen King style. Talking of which, pet cemeteries and pet cremations are now commonplace (about 100,000 per year). Remember, though, if you commit too many resources to your pet's send-off, it might upset elderly relatives if you haven't made similarly extravagant plans for them.

Which brings us to people. There is an industry dedicated to dealing with dead humans. However, this might not be for you. You might be avoiding the law, in which case we don't want to know about it. You will find plenty of reference material on disposal in recent films, such as *Goodfellas* (woodland burial, car boot transportation), *Fargo* (woodchipper) and *Carry on Screaming* (bath of goo). More acceptably, you might not be a murderer, but just feel that the modern undertaking business is over-commercialised and impersonal. Or you might be too tight to pay for a funeral.

You could even find yourself in the situation where no specialists are immediately available, like if you're on a desert island or captive in an isolated farmhouse populated by hillbillies. The important thing is that, unlike washing up, leaving the job until someone else does it isn't an option, especially in summer.

If you want to do your DIY burial legally, you can't just dig a hole and drop Uncle Al in it. There are laws about this sort of thing. First, the authorities who might turn a blind eye to the exact location of your dog's grave are going to be fairly interested if they hear about your uncle's resting place, and local authorities may have special burial guidelines. Second, your neighbours might not like the idea, and might decide you are creating a nuisance or a health hazard, and that means you'll need a lawyer if you want to pull it off. Third, if you want to put up a headstone, mausoleum, folly or ceremonial flagpole, the planning

Here's an idea for you...

If you think coffins are a waste of money and might pollute your garden, why not buy a flat-pack cardboard coffin? We're not making this up. Several places can supply them. 'Manufactured from 98% recycled lumber products ... a white, full overlap lid on an otherwise conventional oblong box shape ... The casket can be painted any design,' it says on this leaflet. We hope you have more luck assembling it than you did with the bookcase you bought last year.

authorities will want to get involved. Finally, if you've got a mortgage, your lender is going to want to know. This is because advertising your house for sale with three bedrooms, two reception rooms and a short walk to the nearest corpse isn't going to get you the asking price.

Depth is also important. The Local Authorities Cemeteries Order 1977 stipulates a minimum depth of three feet for bodies in cemeteries to protect them from 'foraging animals'. Quick, think about something else.

38. Burning the evidence

Modern communications gadgets may offer convenience but they also compromise our privacy. Here's what to do to stop others blundering into your private life via the latest devices in your home.

Defining idea...

'Not every truth is the better for showing its face undisguised.'
PINDAR, Greek poet.

Once upon a time, if you were communicating with someone and preferred to keep it quiet, all you had to do was burn the letter after you'd read it. In this day of mobile phones, email and instant messaging that's become a whole lot more complex.

When the French government first discussed British Telecom's idea of the 1471 code (the number you punch into your phone to see who the last caller was), the debate quickly turned to the subject of wives and mistresses. It was argued that when (not 'if' – this is France, remember) the mistress called, the wife would only need to enter the 'last-caller code' to discover the offending number, even if the mistress had immediately hung up. The debate actually held up the introduction of this facility across the country. As it happens, these worries weren't completely unfounded because 'last call received' is probably second only to unerased text messages and emails as the greatest give-away of our time. So get smart.

We'd like to think you're an honest person but even us honest ones sometimes need discretion in our communications. The Getting Away With It team recommendation is twofold. One, where possible ensure that discrete calls are made from the other person to you and that they always dial the 'number withheld' code before calling. Two, get a second mobile. Inform everyone that it is a work-only phone and that work policy means you have to have a pin code number on it (common company practice these days). Only use that phone. Whatever you do, always manually delete your call records and both incoming and outgoing texts. Not all phones save outgoing messages but it's guaranteed that if you've sent something dodgy then yours will. So, never forget. The other thing is that none of this is worth a damn if you don't keep a

tight hold on your phone bill, so
make sure that it's delivered to a safe
address and destroy or hide as
necessary.

With computers, people tend to
forget that the darned things actually
monitor every single thing you do and
keep a record of it. 'No problem,' we
hear you say, 'I delete everything even
remotely naughty'. Yeah, right. This is
why that's not enough.

When you delete something on a
computer, whether by dragging it to
the 'trash', typing 'del' in DOS (ask your granddad) or selecting and
'deleting' in your mail program then you might think 'job done'
but that's not how it works. The computer doesn't actually delete
the files (nope, not even when you click 'empty recycle bin'),
instead it marks up the disk space they sit on as being free for use
should something else want to be saved there. You can't be sure it's
gone until you delete completely then use the 'compact all folders'
command in Outlook or whatever mail command you had. To be
completely sure, then defragment your hard drive. If using
Windows go to Start, Programs, Accessories, System Tools and there
you'll find Disk Defragmenter and Cleanup utilities.

Here's an idea for you...

So, you're too smart to use email,
preferring instead to use instant
messaging (IM) because that leaves no
trace, right? Ahem. Leaving aside the
fact that the messaging provider
archives the messages, the default of
most systems is to archive your
message history for the session until
you sign out. So make sure you sign
out, and make sure nothing is saved
after that by going to the Preferences
menu and choosing Archive options.
Be sure too that whoever you IM with
does the same otherwise they may be
saving your communications without
knowing it.

When you send a message, a copy of it is added to the 'sent' folder. When you delete that message, a copy will be made in a 'trash' folder so check that the message and its many copies are all gone. If you think you're up against someone who understands how to undelete and recover damaged files (your teenage kids perhaps) then rename a new file with the same name as the old one (including the suffix after the '.') and copy it to the same folder or directory that held the incriminating evidence.

Remember too that most people who get caught out do so because they are simply careless. If there's someone you don't want to be seen communicating with then don't use an electronic address book. Similarly don't ever save their number in your phone. After all, no self-respecting spy would ever write down his or her contacts. If you're opting for discretion then it's time for you to go into James Bond/Mata Hari mode.

39. The perfect alibi

There will always be times in our lives when we are not actually where we say we are. It's a good job that teams of boffins have come up with the cutting edge in alibi technology.

Defining idea...

'People always ask me, "Where were you when Kennedy was shot?" Well, I don't have an alibi.'
EMO PHILIPS, American comedian.

Covering your tracks is essential when being pursued by something big, fierce and equipped with pointy teeth, like the other half, or your boss. Lying is the traditional response to this but to be really convincing you'll need an alibi and this is what modern technology was made for. Welcome to the era of the alibi agency.

You may remember the story of the pub that put its phone in a soundproof booth along with a mini-jukebox into which you'd drop your coin and be rewarded with the sound of typewriters or airport announcements while you phoned. The advance of technology means that this is now within the grasp of us all; indeed, probably literally in your pocket.

In Japan there is a camera phone alibi service that allows you to store a picture of yourself cunningly pasted over a suitable background (on the train, behind the desk, in the Oval Office etc.)

and send it to people, as in 'There you go honey. Now do you believe I'm at work?!' A Romanian company called Simeda has done the same for sound files, allowing subscribers to select from traffic jams, train noises, heavy machinery, or even a dentist's surgery. These then play as background noise during the phone call to back up your story. If you're a chronic liar, it's even possible to assign a selected background track to play automatically when certain numbers call you. Of course, that still takes a certain amount of common sense – your telephonic persecutor may get suspicious after the twentieth time they call and find you're still on the train.

For the full service you're going to need an alibi agency. Alibi agencies offer a range of services from the simple to the complete life screen (bought by the year). Simple alibis might be as basic as an answering service that says you are where you said and promises to pass on the message. The Full Monty will actually make use of real companies and have real secretaries (who themselves don't know you're not a business partner) take the calls. It will also issue business cards and provide a variety of 'colleagues' to call, be seen with, etc.

Moscow-based company Alibi is run by alibi specialist Dmitri Petrov (thinking about it, probably not his real name) and offers a wide variety of convincing ruses. For example, someone who is running out of reasons for repeated absences can have a 'friend' turn up at the house loaded down with fishing gear to drive him off for the weekend. Or a wife looking to get away for a while with no questions asked might be sent a totally convincing looking summons for a court appearance or jury duty in a far away city. A phone number with the summons would be answered by the agency confirming in best bolshy bureaucratese that yes this is indeed the judicial system at work and no she can't get out of it.

Funnily enough, not all alibis are for the reason you were thinking of (oh yes you were). Alibi-Strohmann of Germany tells the story that one of the hardest alibis they ever had to provide was all about blindsiding a girlfriend for two months so that she had no idea her boyfriend was busy … arranging their surprise marriage.

Here's an idea for you...

Looking for a quick get out? Look no further than your phone. One mobile service in the States, for instance, set up a 'Rescue Ring' facility whereby you can have your phone called at a set time to get you out of a corner. The 'Escape-A-Date' service goes a step further and will phone you with a suitable excuse. Your escape mate tells you exactly what to say ('roommate locked out', 'summoned to meeting' etc.) and you just repeat it word for word. Or you could just get a mate to do the job for you – if you trust them that is.

Put your feet up

40. Passing an exam without revising

Spending hours and hours studying, wasting your life – social life at that – all for a piece of paper seems ludicrous, doesn't it? Well perhaps you don't have to.

Defining idea...

'Learning is not compulsory ... neither is survival.'
W. EDWARDS DEMMING

Studying is, at the best of times, an exceptionally dull process. We use so little of what we retain in the real world that it hardly seems worth all the effort. The reality is, of course, we have no choice, unless we fancy ending up on the bap heap, at the bottom of the economic pile, flipping burgers for below-subsistence wages.

Why on earth do they make us study during the summer? When it's hot and sunny all you want to do is chase the opposite sex and frolic in the hay; the last thing on your mind is that all-important exam you have to prepare for. Perhaps it's a government-imposed mechanism for avoiding teen pregnancies. Or maybe it's the sadists in the exam system who want to make your life a misery. (We favour the latter.) So you find yourself in a bit of a bind. On one hand you know you have got to do at least the bare minimum to pass your exams; on the other, you want to escape the thin air of your bedroom. So what can you do to maximise the amount of time you get to play and ensure you do okay in the exams? Well, with the judicious use of a handful of techniques and tools you ought to satisfy your desires while still passing your exams. Of course, the balance you choose to place on both is entirely up to you!

The Getting Away With It team's favourite revision reducers (as we like to call them) are:

- Subliminal learning – who needs books when you can have a few tapes with the key facts on them? After a day's lazing around in the sun, all you have to do is lie on your bed, pop on the Walkman and let your subconscious brain do the work. How's about that for an approach!?

- Use study aids – why reinvent the wheel when you can draw on all the advice and support you need from the experts? A lot of what you need to know for the exam can be condensed into a few pages of text contained within a study guide you can buy for a few pounds.

- Time management – if you can focus your efforts into a couple of hours a day, and we do mean *focus* here, then you can maximise the time you have for fun. It requires the self-discipline of a self-flagellant but without the scarring.

■ Buy some time from someone else – if you are one of these lucky people who have plenty of cash or rich parents who would rather throw money at a problem than deal with it directly, then you are in luck. There are plenty of people out there who will prostitute themselves to get you through the exams: teachers, failed academics and smart-arses desperate for cash. Passing the buck to someone who knows the system is a sure-fire way to reduce the amount of time you need to be spending on revising.

Here's an idea for you...

Make a list of the exam techniques you can think of and decide which ones could offer you the greatest return for the least amount of effort. Certainly give question spotting a go – although it's a bit high risk, so is doing nothing. Once you have got your list, give each technique a try and focus on a small subset that allows you to maximise your frolicking.

■ Tune in to your natural way of learning – yes, we all have preferences, and sadly most of us are oblivious to them. You can waste literally weeks trying to get stuff into your skull to no avail. The simple reason why you fail is that you may have completely missed the way your brain prefers to learn. To absorb as much information as possible, as effortlessly as possible, means that you have to get to the root of how you learn, be it in pictures, words or feelings.

So there you have it, a collection of smart ways you can try out to limit the amount of study time. Don't get too carried away, though. This doesn't mean you can do nothing at all. And remember that spending too much time out in the sun shrivels your skin and gives you cancer, so maybe study is good for you after all.

41. Missing a deadline

From school until retirement, we spend our lives struggling to hit deadlines. And all too often we miss. Missing with panache is the route to a more contented existence.

Defining idea...

'Punctuality is the virtue of the bored.'
EVELYN WAUGH, diary entry, 1962.

Think about it: many of us will be repeatedly missing deadlines for well over half a century. There are only two ways to deal with the situation: do everything on time or try and get away with being late. If you want to achieve the former, take a time management course. Oh, and abandon your plans for the weekend, because you'll be working. If you want to get away with it, read on.

Like the other unsustainable lies we tell ('The cheque's in the post', 'she's just a friend' and 'I was going to pay for it officer, I've no idea how it got into my pocket'), 'I'm just finishing it now, I should have it on your desk by the end of the day' is little more than a delaying tactic. It exists to give us breathing space, but it can't change reality. You are no more likely to get the report on the desk tonight than you are to don a tutu and dance on that desk. The stark truth is this: you will miss your deadline.

Once you have accepted this, there are two tasks you have to achieve: keeping your boss off your back until you do deliver and the creation of an environment that means you will get away with the repercussions of your tardiness.

Succeeding in these tasks grooms you for higher office. We all miss deadlines; it's just that when the blame is handed out, losers catch it and winners don't. Execute the skills below effectively and one day you may be senior enough to set deadlines for other people. At this point, a good understanding of what their excuses are likely to be when they miss those deadlines will be your secret weapon.

When missing deadlines, thorough preparatory work is vital. If you intend to be late, put in a flurry of activity – or what passes for it – as early as possible. Requests for clarification of the brief; regular status reports to people who don't need to know; well-thumbed, clearly labelled files of relevant documents in your in-tray all show that you mean business, while you pop out to the cinema or get away early.

Closer to deadline time, don't hide. You can finesse a few extra days simply by subtly nudging the deadline in casual conversations that you initiate. 'I should have it Wednesday, or Thursday morning at the latest' is followed the next day by 'No problem with Thursday as a delivery day', which commits you to Thursday 5 p.m. With a little effort, you can shunt the delivery into Friday, and once you get to Friday lunchtime, no one expects it until Monday. This very effective way of missing deadlines is known as 'managing expectations'.

Use third parties as fall guys. This relies on what is known as 'workflow', which is defined as 'The ability of other people missing deadlines to make you miss yours'. Don't pretend you don't actually have the information they are supplying, because then someone might check. Instead pretend that you need more time, because you only just got it.

Unexpect the expected. If you know in advance you will be stuck in the usual two-hour traffic queue, keep it to yourself, and then call from the car to say that for some reason you are in a two-hour traffic queue, which is a shame because it means you won't be able to finish the project today. The same goes for meetings that predictably over-run, and if you have to cover for people when you

Here's an idea for you...

Use these deadline-missing excuses when you're not running late, then surprise everyone with a punctual delivery. It means you get a chance to hone your skills in a no-risk situation, and the mild disappointment that your boss feels when you announce you will be late is eclipsed many times over by the delight they feel when you are on time.

knew for weeks they would be out of the office. Practice being sorrowful and surprised. Shrug a bit. Shake your head. Who knew?

Finally, make office alliances. If several of you have to meet the same deadline, make a pact that you are all going to miss it by the same margin. It adds credibility to all the above tactics if you all use them. This also gives you an opportunity: if you agree with your, erm, mates that you will all be three days late, be two days late. It'll seem like you are one day early.

42. I think I'm coming down with something

When you're going to skive off by pretending you aren't well, there are some dos and don'ts to ensure you get sympathy, not the sack. Malinger with merit.

Defining idea...

'The best liar is he who makes the smallest amount of lying go the longest way.'
SAMUEL BUTLER, *The Way of All Flesh*.

Occasionally in our working lives, we need to push on, buck up, be strong and go to work when we don't feel like it because we are 'can do' people. Tips for how to do that are in a different book, because it's statistically more likely that you are a 'can't do' person, and in this

situation you'll need to know how to convincingly fake an illness –
or in GAWI jargon, how to 'throw a sickie'.

People have been throwing sickies ever since there were difficult
jobs that needed to be done which other people could do for you.
As soon as the alpha male in primitive society developed the
language to say, 'Let's go hunting, there's a mammoth out there
with really sharp tusks,' the beta male developed words for 'You go
ahead, I think I'm coming down with a bit of a sniffle'.

Despite having generations of previously unwritten knowledge to
fall back on, the modern worker – that's you – has not learned
many of the principles of throwing a sickie, resulting in some poor
performances. This is one aspect of your job that you simply have
to excel at if you want to get on. If you are unconvincing, your boss
will fire you and your colleagues will hate you. After all, they get to
do the work you are avoiding.

If you only remember one piece of advice, it should be this: keep it
simple. We learn from television shows that some rare diseases are
very spectacular and complicated. Doctors spend years learning
about them, and the five minutes you spent looking up the
symptoms on the Internet are no substitute. Use illnesses with
which you are familiar. When friends, relatives and loved ones are
sick, look on the bright side: when they are better, you will be able
to copy their symptoms and get a few days off as well.

When reporting in for your sickie, do the job yourself. A handy tip is not to speak or drink in the morning before you make the call, especially if you smoke. Your huskiness will be mistaken for laryngitis. Also, make the call from a quiet place. The following are not recommended in this category: train stations, rock concerts, bars. Except when trying to cut the call short (see below) don't put on an act. Ill people play down their symptoms, because they are too ill to make a fuss.

On the other hand, don't undersell your sickness. A common mistake is calling in with something serious because you missed your train or you have a job interview. One hour later, you arrive at the office miraculously cured. A good rule of thumb is that illnesses should last two days, injuries at least one – though don't forget to limp for at least two days afterwards.

Here's an idea for you...

Get in touch with your feelings and don't over-complicate your calls with fancy words. Describe the symptoms that you should be feeling instead of calling in with the name of your supposed condition. Compare 'I just can't stop vomiting ... oh dear, here it comes again ...' with the more usual 'I think I have gastric flu'. Say the first, and no one wants you in the same county. Say the second, and we instinctively assume you are lying.

This raises the final point that separates the amateurs form the professionals. It is highly recommended that you assemble supporting evidence and stay in character. A doctor's certificate may be hard to obtain unless your problem is one of the classic untreatables (think backache), but a spousal alibi is excellent. If your significant other can call later in the day to report that your temperature is still high, you're sleeping now but he or she thought it was best if everyone knew, you are both acting responsibly.

Ultimately, it's not hard to throw a sickie in the short term. It is harder to throw them convincingly over a period of months or years. Think of this strategically: cycle your ailments, keep a log, recruit friends to support your arguments. And keep watching those hospital TV shows for your raw material: every actor who plays a patient in them is throwing a sickie. If they can, you can.

43. Doing nothing at work – bosses

Like the muddy tropical river to the hippo, or the lush rainforest to the sloth, middle management is the natural environment of choice for the serious slacker.

Defining idea...

'If you get to be thirty-five and your job still involves wearing a name tag, you've probably made a serious vocational error.'
DENNIS MILLER, US football coach.

Skiving and slacking on low-paid, unrewarding 'McJobs' is understandable but a worrying sign of a lack of ambition and imagination. Smarter loafers don't even consider this course, preferring instead to hone their idling skills in a reasonably well-paid job in management.

A survey by Investors in People recently found that 84% of workers in organisations with more than 1,000 employees thought they had a lazy colleague. That compared with only 50% in companies with fewer than fifty staff. There are many ways of explaining that figure, including the fact that smaller companies inspire more loyalty and have fewer places to hide. More precisely, it probably comes down to the simple truth that small companies don't have middle management.

In France there was an outrage over Corinne Maier's book *Hello Laziness* (*Bonjour Paresse*) and its subtitle, *The Art and the Importance of Doing the Least Possible in the Workplace*. Ms Maier's main point was that most 'work' is pointless posturing, politics and meeting mania and so the only real response was to go with the flow and do the least possible. To your savvy slacker, this will have been very old news. Maier's suggestion that the best rewards come from 'the most useless sort of job ... consultant, expert, or adviser' might make a couple of consultants feel uneasy but hardly come as a shock to anyone who has ever set foot in any company big enough to have an atrium. So how do you get yourself into this skiving sweet spot? Simple. You're going to need two main things: charm and a team of other people to do the work for you.

Really top-notch loafing requires teamwork: the team does the work, you do the loafing. The key to that is making sure that the people who actually work closest to you see that it's in their interest to protect you. To do that you're going to have to weave that magic charm on them, let them know you're on their side, and that you have the key to their future happiness. If you don't have a hope in hell of pulling that one off, then it's equally effective (though harder to achieve) to let them know that you have the key to their very best skeleton closets. Since the best skeletons tend to be hidden safely beyond the reach of the full-time layabout, then the first option is the best and that means that you will have to put a bit of effort into getting your staff grades, salaries, and perks above the norm. It may sound like hard work but in the long run you'll be doing yourself a favour. A team in line is half the job done.

Here's an idea for you...

To really make the grade as a slacker boss, you will need a 'treasure' – an assistant who actually does some of the things you should do, keeps your boss at bay and also enjoys an excellent work environment. In many companies the treasure is so well respected that other managers eventually don't bother approaching the slacker (that's you) at all. Tread carefully, though, because lots of slackers are rumbled and the ones that lose their jobs are those who have lost the trust of their treasure. Fail to ensure your treasure gets what they need, or start to act Ab Fab, sweetie, and you're on a hiding to hard work.

Truly accomplished slackers then ensure that they spend a vast amount of time with clients/on the road/etc. to explain their prolonged absence. Be careful about the old 'working from home' ruse – it suggests that there will be evidence of work done, and that is never the object. Team building, client relationships, and marketing are much safer bets for spending days out of the building without anyone expecting you to have anything to show for it.

One other word of advice: for every top-drawer loafer, there is a nemesis, usually in the form of an ambitious colleague eager to get on, possibly at your expense. This inspires panic in substandard slackers, who may be galvanised into extreme responses, even including doing some work. Don't fall into this trap. The fact is that the average ambitious middle manager spends less than two years in the same job so if you've got it sweet then don't move on and start again; instead, sit tight and look to your team, not to your new threat.

44. Doing nothing at work – employees

For run-of-the-mill workers, the key to loafing is to create an illusion of purpose and industry that deflects the scrutiny of superiors.

Defining idea...

'Look at me: I worked my way up from nothing to a state of extreme poverty.'
GROUCHO MARX

The late, great Spike Milligan used to tell a tale of his army years, during which one inspired loafer took to wandering around with a tin of DDT (insecticide). If ever anyone challenged him to explain what he was doing he snapped sharply to attention and replied 'de-lousing sir'. Nobody ever enquired further and he would be free to carry on doing precisely nothing in peace.

We're not saying that you should take to schlepping around large containers of poison (although this may still work in the military, prisons, and fast-food outlets) but the key points to this technique are as true today as they ever were. The first is that if you want to spend all day doing sweet Fanny Adams then you'd better have a cover story. The second is that whatever that story is you must be prepared to launch into it with conviction and the kind of enthusiasm that suggests nothing would please you more than to explain it in incomprehensible detail until your interrogator's ears bleed.

When it comes to a cover story there's nothing like a good prop and we've come a long way from the DDT tin. Today's loafers have at their fingertips an armoury of high-tech tools.

Once the great trick was to always be seen with a clipboard. Clipboards speak volumes about business, importance, and those endless 'jobs' like 'stocktaking' and 'time and motion studies' that were always nothing more than the inventions of loafers looking to do as little as possible before knocking-off time came around again. The trusty clipboard (and its executive brother, the bulging file) can still come in handy but if you really want to get away with it these days it's time to go digital. Digital devices add a whole new dimension to loafing because their very presence intimidates the Luddites and their multi-tasking flexibility makes it hard for even the initiate to call your bluff. Proof positive of this is the evolution of the uber-loafer – the king of the freeloading food chain. Posing as 'systems administrator', 'network engineer' or any one of a dozen similarly meaningless monikers, these geek gods have reached the noodling nirvana where they can face down anybody from line managers to

Here's an idea for you...

Get yourself a key friend in geekdom. Someone savvy on the systems side is needed to tell you crucial info such as whether the company has keystroke monitoring systems to record effort and detect games players. Bunking off to see a systems person is also a universally accepted ploy, even in the future. It's reassuring to note that in the high-tech futuristic vision *The Island*, Ewan McGregor regularly shouts 'computer down' and slides off to see his mate Steve Buscemi in tech support. Note also that the long-term result of this behaviour is that he gets to hang out on yachts and shack up in a playboy mansion with Scarlett Johannson.

the CEO. This is done with nothing more than a withering look and a sarcastic outpouring of gobbledygeek. A typical example would go as follows:

Baffled CEO/MD/HR exec: 'So what exactly have you been doing for the last three weeks?'

Uber-loafer [sighing at the pathetic inadequacy of the question/questioner]: 'Patching the Unix kernel.'

CEO/MD/HR exec [even more baffled]: 'Patching the colonel?'

Uber-loafer [with the exaggerated patience normally reserved for small children]: 'Upgrade, protocol, security, TCP/IP, parallel-processing, cluster, hacker, hexadecimal, three-speed, cupcakes …" [the final words of which are normally delivered to the back of an already retreating questioner].

You don't have to be an uber-loafer to take a leaf from their book. Even the humblest warehouse worker, if wielding one of those brilliant, handheld data input devices, is in a position of strength because nobody, not even the person who bought them, really knows all the things you might be doing with them. Other examples include Blackberries ('of course I'm not skiving; can't you see I'm emailing?'), laptops ('Fragfest? All-out Hover Tank war? Certainly not; it's a 3D graphic representation of next-year's projected margins'), or any kind of spreadsheet (make sure you can bring up an elaborate diagrammatic representation with a triumphant punch of the button).

45. Working by the pool

OK, maybe not by the pool, but at least earn your salary from your kitchen. Other people work from home, so why not you?

For an ever-growing chunk of the population, working from home isn't a euphemism for skiving; it's a way of life. They've cut out that hour-long commute, the grumpy boss hovering over your shoulder, office dress policy, and sandwiches at the keyboard for lunch.

Defining idea...

'Important principles may and must be flexible.'
ABRAHAM LINCOLN

For a start if you have kids under the age of six (or eighteen if they have a disability) and you have been working for a company for 26 weeks or more then you have the automatic right to apply to work flexibly. The idea is that you then have more time to spend taking care of your kids, but that could mean many things: for example, you could be applying to start work later so as to be able to take the kids to school, or to start earlier and finish earlier so as to be there to pick them up after school. It could also mean working at home a certain number of days a week.

Employers have a statutory duty to 'consider the applications seriously' and must follow a specific procedure when considering them, which means that they can't refuse you without giving precise reasons. So head them off at the pass by sitting down and putting together a killer application that can't be refused. What you will need to think about is the benefit to the company, not to you. Try to:

- Explain how you will make up exactly the same time so the company isn't losing anything.

- Point out that you will be more motivated and happy with your new timetable, and therefore more productive.

- Show that the company may stand to make savings in the office environment (perhaps they could do away with your desk or give your office workstation to someone else).

- Demonstrate that you have the appropriate technology and abilities to do your job from home (this may mean researching Voice over Internet Protocol (VoIP) telephony, for example, to handle phone diversions at no extra cost).

- Consider means of monitoring your performance that can be used to prove you are reaching agreed levels and so back up your claim to be more productive with the new timetable.

Your boss has 28 days from receiving the request to arrange a meeting with you and explore your proposal in depth. Fourteen days after that, the employer must write to you to either agree the new pattern and a start date or else provide clear business grounds as to why your proposal is unworkable. If that's the case, the letter also has to set out the appeal procedure for you to contest the decision. For more details take a look at the DTI website (www.dti.gov.uk).

When you're putting together your proposal you should consider how much experience your company already has of flexible working. Bear in mind that you may be seen as setting a precedent and so you are effectively establishing the benefits of flexible working in general to a company that may not yet be convinced about it. In that case, make doubly sure that you have the facts and figures at your fingertips and can explain how they would affect the company.

Here's an idea for you...

As part of the flexible working legislation you have the right to take a colleague with you when meeting the boss to discuss your proposal. So instead of reinventing the wheel seek out others in the company who have successfully applied for flexible working and get them on your side. A little flattery goes a long way and, after all, you are saying 'I want to be like you'. They in turn have already got good arguments for their (your) case: they can hardly sit there and admit that it doesn't work and all they do is slack off on company time.

An interesting stat to bear in mind is that, according to the Equal Opportunities Commission, 80% of women return to work within

17 months of childbirth, but only 47% return to the same employer. By contrast, employers who offer flexible working patterns have return rates of 90%, saving the business replacement costs and retaining valuable skills and experience.

Finally, very few companies study their own productivity levels, and even fewer publish their findings. BT does both and found that home workers were actually 31% more efficient than their office counterparts. The happy worker, it seems, really is a more productive worker.

46. Winging a meeting

There's a good reason why we don't prepare for meetings: we don't have time. Seriously. Don't bother.

The Wharton Center for Applied Research recently found that the average senior executive spends 23 hours a week in meetings, and the more senior you are the worse it gets. If we prepared for meetings properly, there wouldn't be enough time left in the day to hold them. And if we did all

Defining idea...

'Meetings are held because men seek companionship, or, at a minimum, wish to escape the tedium of solitary duties.'
J. K. GALBRAITH, economist, in *The Great Crash*.

the preparation and called all the people we should have done, chances are we would have solved the problem already, rendering the meeting even more useless than it already is.

Yet convention demands that when attending a meeting you look like you have put in some work, especially if you called it. If you are in charge, the most important thing about running a meeting is to create a detailed agenda. Don't worry: we didn't say a new agenda, just a detailed one. Keep a standard agenda template: comments from last meeting, unresolved issues, input from departments/working groups/key contributors, suggestions for next steps, any other business and date of next meeting. Then all you have to do is add the correct date, the title of the meeting and the names of people who you want to speak against each item. This name is never you. The other attendees will be so busy looking for their initials that they won't spot that it is the same agenda as last time.

Always allocate precise times to each item on the agenda, but make no effort to enforce these times.

The easiest way to control a meeting without contributing is to emphasise that you are listening. Remember, listening is good, because listening means not doing. If your agenda looks too short, invite someone, preferably on a mobile phone, to conference call in to the meeting. Connecting and reconnecting will swallow at least 45 minutes of the available time, and you can always shout 'What do you think, Derek?' down the line if you're in a tight spot.

If you are not running the meeting, but expect to be named on the list of people who will contribute content, the important thing is to convince everyone that you have a lot to say while saying as little as possible. Bring a long typed list (any typed list will do as long as it consists of at least ten points) to every meeting. Don't let anyone else see the detail on it. When it's your turn, pick it up and scan carefully. Hearts will sink until you check your watch, glance at the agenda, and say: 'In the interests of time, I'll skip most of this, and just cover a few essential points.' Your diligence, humility and ability to prioritise will attract admiration from people who don't know that you are holding your shopping list.

Here's an idea for you...

If you want to arrive late and/or leave early, keep one of those small suitcases with wheels on it and bring it to the meeting. Quietly park it in plain view. A late arrival means you just got off a plane or train. An early departure means that you really have to get to the airport or station right away. Your very presence will seem like you're doing everyone a favour.

In any meeting designed to decide something, there will usually be The Expert, the one person who knows what he or she is talking about. It would have been much better for everyone if The Expert had been allowed to get on with making the decision alone, but it's important to have a meeting so that you can contribute by agreeing with everything he or she says, and maybe steal some of the credit as a result. Accomplish this by identifying that meeting's Expert, preferably on the way in to the meeting, and engage in friendly banter, which might reveal what point of view The Expert holds. If possible sit opposite The Expert – this allows you to exchange knowing looks, raised eyebrows and vigorous nods on cue. The Expert's aura of capability will extend to you. If it's time for a comment, try 'As [insert name of Expert] says...' or 'I agree with...' Don't do this too often, though: everyone hates a kiss-ass, and if you're too vocal, you will be given things to do, which isn't the idea at all.

Mind over matter

47. Gamesmanship

True cheating is not the way to win at sports because the detection-risk is very high – anathema to the Getting Away With It team. Instead try gamesmanship.

Defining idea...

'How to make the other man feel that something has gone wrong, however slightly.'
STEPHEN POTTER, defining lifemanship.

Stephen Potter, the godfather of Getting Away With It, once described gamesmanship as being the art of beating your opponents without actually cheating. This comes down to a number of sneaky but not illegal tricks of wrangling the situation so that your opponent starts out with the disadvantage of being bothered, irritated, angry, and generally (literally and metaphorically) playing with the sun in their eyes. It's easier to do than you might think.

Try this with a friend. Tell them that all they have to do is to talk 'normally' for a minute. Take turns. Chances are you'll end up giggling at the idiocy of it and just how stilted you sound yourself when you try it. It's because we suddenly lose the fluidity of a natural action when we have to focus on it. Filmmakers will tell you that it is nigh on impossible to get someone to walk up to the camera without freezing or striding with all the naturalness of an Action Man. If you've ever seen a cheap local cinema ad in which the owner of a garage chews his way through a one-line endorsement, you'll recognise the syndrome. Quite simply if we focus on it too much we can lose the ability to walk or talk smoothly, so what do you think it does to the sportsman?

There are many ways of unleashing the savage weapon that is self-awareness, ranging from the way you dress to the briefest of comments. Turning up badly dressed is a wonderful wile because it works on a number of levels. Firstly it encourages people to underestimate you, which is always an advantage, but more importantly it makes them suddenly aware of what they look like themselves. Someone who shows up in an old school sports kit or something clearly borrowed and ancient is saying 'I never really play this sport', which by comparison immediately makes their properly kitted-out opponent look like they take it far too seriously and may even be an 'all the gear, no idea' wannabe. It only takes one successful rally/shot/move from the opponent in the rags to make the other look a fool and, more importantly, feel

Here's an idea for you...

If you're going to unleash the weapon of self-awareness then you will need a good strategy yourself. Try 'dinking'. Dinking originally came from tennis but is applicable to all racket games and the spirit applies to any sport. A dinker doesn't try any fancy shots, but instead just returns the ball/shuttlecock every time and waits for the better player to lose their rag or overreach themselves. Big hitters wear themselves out trying to get a winning shot against the dinker who doggedly refuses to risk anything other than a stolid return. It's particularly good after you've irritated your opponent in a minor but niggling way.

one. Combine that with the ignoble art of 'dinking' (see opposite) and you have a lethal combination for winding up far superior opposition.

The other technique for unleashing self-awareness is the way you talk to your opponent. Compliments can be double-edged, even lethal if used properly. Emile Zatopek, the legendary distance runner, famously came to prominence by turning to the then champion mid race and asking him if they were running at a fast enough pace. Flustered the champion replied 'no', sped up, lost his timing, and with it the race. In a similar vein the compliment of death can be applied in almost any one-to-one sport. Try this when next playing golf/squash/polo. Go up to your opponent and say in terms of obvious admiration 'that was a superb shot – could you show me just where you placed your hands to achieve that?' In showing you, they will have to think about something they've probably never thought about before. It will be a small miracle if they manage to reproduce that shot in a hurry.

The beauty of gamesmanship is that, unlike cheating, it can be done in the open, and can even work if the opponent is aware that that's exactly what you're playing at.

48. Being more gorgeous than you really are

Getting away with anything is largely about confidence. Looking gorgeous is no exception. Here's how to achieve the wow factor whenever you make your entry.

Defining idea...

'Charm: It's a sort of bloom on a woman. If you have it, you don't need to have anything else; and if you don't have it, it doesn't much matter what else you have.'
J. M. BARRIE, writer.

The Getting Away With It team once worked with an editor who has extraordinary charisma. She has something, an aura, that makes people notice her wherever she goes. She's attractive and tall, which always helps, but she also exudes charm: a mixture of friendliness, warmth plus a kind of X factor that goes beyond the merely physical.

How does she do it? Okay, she's one of the lucky ones – her charisma is innate. However, we in the Team believe you can approach it methodically.

Let's look at what the experts say about first impressions. Well, apparently 55% of the impact we make depends on how we look and behave, 38% on how we speak and only 7% on what we actually say. That's great news for the Eliza Doolittles among us, but it gives all of us something to work on.

Always dress the part

Think of that foxy pink, slinky dress in which you never fail to 'pull'. Great party cracker, but it'll do you no favours at that board meeting. So the first rule of successful first impressions is to always keep the occasion uppermost in your mind and dress accordingly. That goes for make-up, jewellery, fragrance and shoes as well as the clothes.

There's a chilling tale of one young woman who strayed from the acceptable path of 'navy, below-the-knee only skirt suits' that were the uniform for women who wanted to be taken seriously in the City investment bank in which she worked. Always wanting to steal the limelight and turn heads, one morning she apparently sashayed into her prim, stuffy, grey office in a pair of voluminous, bottom-caressing, silky flared trousers. Big mistake. Rather than having the desired effect, which was to elicit desire, her boss gave her a public dressing down for 'coming to work in pyjamas – and looking ridiculous'.

While you may condemn the anachronistic attitude that keeps women asexual in men's suits, learn from it. Always wear what's appropriate for the occasion. You'll feel more confident if you know you're looking suitably business like/smartly casual/glamorous. Your overall appearance is the first thing that will be noticed.

Be comfortable

Hot date? Big swanky black tie party? Shopping for a new outfit for an exciting 'do' is part of the pleasure. But you'll be more confident if you're comfortable. So, always break in new shoes, practise with underwear (that revealing chiffon number may expose more than you'd bargained for, other outfits may require a thong, etc.), even road-test jewellery if you're allergic to certain metals.

But KNOW you look amazing

Spend as long as you can afford preparing. Promising new date? Splurge on a blow dry. Big party? Get a manicure or facial. Pampering yourself makes you feel more attractive instantly, which makes you more confident. And that shows.

Here's an idea for you...

Prep before the big moment. Get a little photo album and fill it with pix of yourself looking your best. When you need a boost, get it out – look at it and realise you're not bad, not bad at all... While you're doing that, try an aromatherapy upper. Essential oil of bergamot is said to increase self-esteem and grapefruit can be refreshing and revitalising. Try wallowing in an aromatherapy infused bath before you head off, or pop a few drops on a tissue and inhale deeply two or three times en route to the event.

EXPECT to be liked

A good way to offset nerves, anxiety, even dread about meeting people is to rehearse: imagine yourself making that great first impression. Repeat to yourself, 'I will shine tonight/today. I always live up to expectations. I'm friendly. People like me. I look fantastic.'

The first hello

Perfect a firm, confident handshake – making eye contact as you do so, which is vital. Smile and look happy. The impact will be immediate and you'll generate warmth and friendliness. People like people who like them – and a smile is an instant signal that you do.

Slow down

Nerves can turn even the most mellifluous voiced siren into a gabbling Minnie Mouse on helium. Stop. Relax. Make a point of trying to talk slowly (go down a couple of octaves). Breathe deeply, walk slowly and carefully, maintain eye contact, however nervous you're feeling. Smile and laugh as much as possible (again, when appropriate). You'll automatically exude confidence.

Rehearse your chat

Never know what to talk about? Do your homework. If it's a scary meeting, research topics that are pertinent to the people you know you'll be meeting – the region they're from, what's going on in the news, etc. Alternatively, encourage the other person to do the talking. Ask them about themselves – how they got there, how they know the host – and show an interest in them. And look for common ground – holidays in France, mutual friends. It's an instant way to get the conversation flowing. Perfect a few conversational ice-breakers. A good, easy-to-remember conversation booster is FORE. So stick to topics such as family, occupation, relaxation and education.

49. Beach beauty – looking good half naked

Oh, to look gorgeous half naked without surgery. Well, with the right attitude and a few beauty essentials, you can display your wares with pride in no time.

Defining idea...

'How to look thin on the beach? Pick a spot where the sand is dry and uneven and hollow out two leg-sized areas. Position your towel or sarong over the furrows, place a leg in each one and admire the fact that gravity prevents your thighs from spreading horizontally.'
SARAH BARCLAY, author of Beauty SOS, Carlton Books.

You know how it is. You book that week somewhere hot and exotic, then dream of sashaying down the beach, conch in hand, wearing next to nothing and a come-hither smile. You're toned, bronzed, stylish in a half-naked way, and would make Bo Derek/Brad Pitt look homely.

Fast forward to day two of the holiday and you're lobster pink, sore and have hair the texture of tumbleweed. If you're a bloke, you've already given up on holding your gut in and you're skulking at the bar.

How is it the Italians and the French look naturally amazing on the beach? One of the GAWI team recalls sitting, white and pasty, on an exclusive resort in Sardinia surrounded by scantily clad Mediterranean goddesses. Her husband's head snapped back and forth with such alacrity it seemed traction might be called for. Even the Olive Oyl look-alikes looked amazing; they somehow – *somehow* – pulled off sex appeal in heels, a diamante thong and white leather sun-visors. Every bloke, likewise, walked like a stud even if realistically they were either overweight or undertall, depending on how you look at it.

The secret, quite apart from the fact Mediterraneans are blessed with olive skin that tans like a warm nut, is that they prime, protect, accessorise – and wear very little with *confidence*.

So before you take anything off, think smooth skin, flattering swimwear and barely-there make up. Most of all, imagine yourself as a beach babe or sand stud. Then follow these few simple beach rules.

Girls

Never forget hair removal: And do it in advance – no eleventh-hour hacking away at your bikini line or underarms with a disposable razor in your hotel room. Experts swear waxing is the best option. Get it done two or three days before you fly, and avoid hot baths afterwards or the follicles will turn bright red and take longer to calm down. If your skin becomes inflamed and irritated, hydrocortisone cream's a great way to calm it.

Get baby-soft skin: Invest in a good body exfoliator, and apply it with circular movements to boost circulation. A cheaper option is Epsom salts, which will help to deep-cleanse your skin. Just fill a cup with salts and add enough water to make a paste. Massage over skin, then rinse off. Always moisturise after exfoliating. Leave the moisturiser on for about 15 minutes before you apply your fake tan (see below) so it doesn't interfere with the active ingredient in fake tanning products.

Perfect your fake tan: A tan can hide flab, cellulite, and make your limbs look instantly longer. Get a fake one before you get there but remember you still need the suntan cream as a fake tan won't protect your skin.

Here's an idea for you...

Focus on your feet. Ideally, book a pre-holiday salon pedicure. For a quickie at-home job, apply a foot scrub, rinse, then smother your feet in foot cream and wrap them in a towel or plastic bag for five to ten minutes before rinsing. Stained toe nails? Try dissolving a couple of denture cleansing tablets in a glass of water, dip your nailbrush into it and gently scrub your nails, then rinse with warm water before finishing off with nail varnish.

Prime beach hair: Use a deep conditioning treatment once a week for a month or so before you head off on holiday. Once you're there, substitute your regular shampoo and conditioner for specialist sun products. And on the beach? If your hair is fine, stick to gels. Creams are good for protecting curly, wiry or thicker hair. A chignon is easy to wear, or try a scarf or bandana. Don't get your highlights done before the holiday – the sun and chlorine will interfere with the colour. Instead get a great haircut that will look good wet or dry.

Guys
Read the above. No, really: give it a bit of thought because you too could do with a hairless back, bronze tan and good-looking hair. Just remember to lie to your dying day that you ever did.

Don't even think about white swimwear, and go for surfers' board shorts rather than Speedos – they hide so much more yet still look cool.

Don't try to pull your stomach in when posing by the pool – it will leave you struggling to breathe and your buttocks clenched like you've got a £50 note held between them. Instead of suck in, try to tense your stomach muscles – you can keep it up longer, it actually builds muscle tone, and you can still breathe and talk.

50. Playing politics – and winning

Show us someone who says they're not interested in office politics and we'll show you someone who's not going up the organisation as far as their talent deserves.

Defining idea...

'If the devil doesn't exist, but man has created him, he has created him in his own image and likeness.'
FEDOR DOSTOEVSKY

Good office politicians keep the competition, their management and colleagues on the back foot by never accepting the existing organisation as it is. Two great ways to win here – abolish your job and/or create a completely new one.

Promotions never come as fast as the GAWI person wants. The organisation settles down, your boss is comfortable with your performance but has no intention of promoting you because, you know, they'll have to find a replacement. And they certainly don't want you to get their job.

The time has come for you to play some office politics and make that new job happen. After all, you need to do more than survive in this area.

Job description, what job description?

One of the things you can do is to make your job redundant. This
may seem a risky process, but it's a great mistake in career
planning to assume that the current management structure is the
one in which you have to succeed. Indeed the opposite is the case
– and you'll probably get away with it.

Here's the reasoning. Many jobs exist because they have always
done so, rather than because they represent the best way of
getting things done successfully. If you go into a new job and do
it the best way for your organisation to succeed, you'll probably
find yourself going way outside the original job description. So,
your way of operating gets better results. Now delegate as much
of the job as you can in your new way of working and guess what.
When you explain what has happened to your boss, he or she will
realise that they need to change the structure of their operation.
If you've done this ploy well, they'll also realise that your tasks
are now handled much more efficiently and they don't need you
in your old role. You've got away with it. Time to move onwards
and upwards.

The fundamental lesson here is to use your influence and authority
to get the best results possible without paying much attention to
how things were done in the past.

Oh, the obvious person for the job seems to be me

The corollary of abolishing your job, namely inventing a new one, also holds true. People who succeed are the ones who help the organisation keep up to date and help to prevent it ossifying.

It is easier to create a new job if the change helps the organisation achieve better performance, but it's possible to do it for your own purposes alone. Probably started by putting up an unsolicited paper, the creation of a new job is in two parts. First describe the new way of doing business that will ensure that the job of your dreams is going to exist. Then sell the idea. What you're doing here is showing what your new plan will do in business terms rather than in structural or people terms. Don't reveal your whole hand at this stage because it's too early. Don't give anyone the opportunity to say that what you're doing is for your own greater glory rather than the advancement of the organisation. Having sold the change, produce your implementation plan and, of course, include the new positions required.

Here's an idea for you...

Look around at how you and your colleagues work. Now ask yourself this question: 'If I owned this business, what changes would I make to my part of the organisation to make a big improvement?' This should give you loads of ammunition to put up a paper that suggests the changes which sensibly should be made. Now you're off and running towards inventing and then taking the new job that you really want.

Next, it's time to go for it. Do not at this stage play any kind of shrinking violet game; clearly show that you are the person for the promoted role you've chosen and defined. You have the business benefits behind you and they have been agreed, so tell people that you should have the job. Make sure, by the way, the new job description has all the elements needed for your next step – access to senior management and a high profile when required. The risk and return on getting away with this career procedure will be very good if you've got it right. After all, you've moulded a job where the circumstances and your skills will be a perfect fit.

51. Breaking off a relationship

Dumping your partner is traumatic for sensitive souls, so we procrastinate. This usually means we do it in grim instalments. With the right mind-set there's a better way.

At the minimum, dumping involves gruesome conversations during which tears mingle with you awkwardly mumbling 'sorry, sorry, sorry,' and staring at your feet for what seems like three

Defining idea...

Reverend Lovejoy: 'Get a divorce.'
Marge: 'But isn't that a sin?'
Reverend Lovejoy: 'Marge, just about everything's a sin. [Holds up Bible] Ever sat down and read this thing? Technically we're not supposed to go to the bathroom.'
THE SIMPSONS

years. At worst, it can lead to raised voices in the pub as you hiss 'Can't we talk about the thing with your brother/sister/ grandmother later? It was New Year! I was on antibiotics!' People you never met stare at you thinking 'You bastard! How could you?!'

If you had known the break-up was going to be like this, you might not have got into the relationship in the first place. However, we're betting it won't stop you from being in the same situation a few months later. That's why it is vital to have some pain-free strategies for finishing a relationship cleanly and leaving unscathed, for everyone's sake. Actually, mostly for yours.

This is not unnatural or unethical. You used low cunning to get into the relationship in the first place, so why not use the same ability to get out of it? Think of it as a negative chat-up line.

Rule one (of one): get on with it. Don't listen to those people who advise taking the easy way out, either by just not returning calls and hoping that someone gets the hint or, even worse, going into hiding. That's just putting off the evil deed. And don't take the chicken's way out and ditch the partner by text message (not that this stopped 9% of us from dumping a partner by SMS this year – 20% among 15 to 24 year olds). The danger is that you'll get into one of those interminable back-and-forth text exchanges that can last longer than the relationship. Email is worse. Your ex will forward the mail to everyone who knows you, and you'll never cop off with his or her friends ever again. Considering this is probably one of the reasons you wanted to break up to start with, that's poor thinking.

So, do it in person. There's only one location to do the deed: at his/her place. This means your ex can tell you to get out RIGHT NOW, which may be the first time in months that you've wholeheartedly agreed on what to do next.

Set yourself a time limit for discussion, measured in minutes, not days. Get right down to business, but avoid clichés. 'It's not you, it's me…' isn't fooling anyone. 'I love you, but I'm not in love with you,' 'I need some space,' and 'It's nobody's fault' are just twaddle, passing time until the sobbing/shouting/glass throwing starts. This is one of the few times in a relationship that it's okay to talk solely about yourself. If you say 'I hate the way you eat', your soon-to-be-ex can offer to change their eating habits. If you say, 'I wake up every morning hating you,' there's no obvious counter offer.

Here's an idea for you...

Don't set the whole dumping thing up over time by saying 'We need to talk', 'Let's get together sometime and see where we stand', that sort of thing. This isn't going to help get the whole thing done without recrimination. Always remember, speed and efficiency are best for both of you. Surgeons don't remove an appendix by spending two weeks prodding the area with a scalpel to see what happens.

If the relationship is obviously boring and tetchy, you can attempt mutuality, as in 'We both know …'. This wins you kudos for honesty, which can speed you through to the end credits. Your ex can also feel that he or she was as much the dumper as the dumpee, and can tell all your friends that it wasn't your idea, which is a small price to pay.

Finally, be generous. It's over, but let him or her know that some element of it has been fantastic. Emphasise that this fantasticness is now past tense. Don't carry this complimenting thing too far: goodbye sex is a very, very bad idea in all cases.

If all else fails try one or more of the following: move to Albania; grow a moustache and change your name; take out a restraining order; frame your ex for a serious crime; change your sexuality; change your sex.

52. Go bald gracefully

Getting away with going bald is an important life skill for men. You'll need a frame of mind in which reality shines through and acceptance is your goal. Tough it out.

If you become a baldy badly, schoolchildren will throw stones at you

Defining idea...

'We're all born bald, baby.'
TELLY SAVALAS

'A man can be short and dumpy and getting bald, but if he has fire, women will like him.'
MAE WEST

and relatives will look at photographs of you whenever they want a good laugh. You don't want that.

The only men who don't worry about their hair falling out are the ones who have already lost it – which amounts to around three in ten men approaching the end of their thirties. The other seven are loudly making jokes about how their friends are getting a bit thin on top while anxiously checking the mirror and secretly eyeing the shampoo shelf in the supermarket for the bottle that promises extra volume.

It is important to accept that everyone has already noticed. It doesn't matter how carefully you have been combing to hide your bald spot, or how often you have avoided windy days, remember that the only person denied a really good look at the top and back of your head is you. Everyone else caught on to the fact you are losing your thatch long before you did.

Your motto should be: hide nothing. For example, when you start to feel the crown of your head pressing against your fingers, it's natural to comb your hair a little more carefully. Soon, you're avoiding going out in the rain. Your barber notices what you're doing, and leaves that area a little longer. You start to experiment with hair products that keep this piece of hair in place. You set your alarm twenty minutes earlier so you can reattach your hair using hairspray. Then one day, a few years later, you realise that you have turned into Bobby Charlton.

During this time you fooled precisely nobody, and all those hours in front of the mirror are hours you will never have back.

Many men believe that women don't like bald men. This is not true. Women don't like flabby, sweaty, ignorant, self-obsessed men who love their cars more than they love their girlfriends. Compared with this, the exact amount of hair you have on your head is a mere detail. This means that if you're worried that no hair means no girlfriend, the first step towards getting away with encroaching baldness should be a visit to the gym and the launderette, where you can fix the more urgent problems that you can do something about.

Step two: get a decent haircut. Less is more. The closer your remaining hair is to your head, the less different it looks to the bits where there isn't hair: think Bruce Willis. Having your hair clipped short actually makes you look like you have more hair, not less – or just stops people looking, because there's no furtive bald spot to seek out. It also has time management benefits because you'll no longer have to carefully arrange your hair every morning. Haircuts are cheap and take five minutes. Plus you don't have to waste time and money on conditioner, because you don't need to use it.

Step three: groom well. Use the extra time liberated by your new hairstyle to think about the other nine tenths of your body. If you have thick tufts springing from your ears, nose and back, your loved ones will not treat this as compensation for the lack of hair on your head, so clip and wax. Also, you may have noticed that girlfriends have entire wardrobes of clothes with which they attempt to accentuate the bits of themselves that they like, and draw attention away from the bits they don't. They're on to something here; after all, they fooled you with it.

Always remember that, men – male pattern baldness is the price we pay for getting the better deal on almost everything else in life, so stop whining and hiding your head. Don't even think about hair transplants and weaves and liquids that cost £30 a month. Even if they might do something to begin with, they'll stop working as soon as you stop buying them. If baldness is good enough for Sean Connery, frankly it's good enough for you.

Here's an idea for you...

Don't wear a hat everywhere because you don't want people to know you're going bald. It's like attaching a flashing sign to your head saying 'embarrassed bald man'. What did you think when you saw that guy today wearing a hat for no obvious reason? You thought, 'He's going bald'. We rest our case.

Where it's at...